INSIGHT FOR LIVING

—— **Broadcast Schedule** ——

Memorable Scenes from Old Testament Homes

March 26–April 23, 2001

Monday	**March 26**	**The Son Who Couldn't Win** *Genesis 25:19–34; 26:34–28:9*
Tuesday	**March 27**	**The Son Who Couldn't Win**
Wednesday	**March 28**	**The Son Who Couldn't Win**
Thursday	**March 29**	**The Farmer Who Murdered His Brother** *Genesis 4:1–15*
Friday	**March 30**	**The Farmer Who Murdered His Brother**

Monday	**April 2**	**The Patriarch Who Lost It All** *Job 1–2; 42:7–17*
Tuesday	**April 3**	**The Patriarch Who Lost It All**
Wednesday	**April 4**	**The Father Who Released His Son** *Genesis 22:1–14*
Thursday	**April 5**	**The Father Who Released His Son**
Friday	**April 6**	**The Boy Who Heard God's Voice** *1 Samuel 3:1–18*

Monday	**April 9**	**The Boy Who Heard God's Voice**

Easter Messages

Tuesday	**April 10**	**You and Me, and Gethsemane** *Luke 22:39–46*
Wednesday	**April 11**	**You and Me, and Gethsemane**
Thursday	**April 12**	**From Tombstone to Triumph** *Selected Scriptures*
Friday	**April 13**	**From Tombstone to Triumph**

Memorable Scenes from Old Testament Homes

(continued)

Monday	**April 16**	**The Teenager Who Whipped a Giant** *1 Samuel 17:1–54*
Tuesday	**April 17**	**The Teenager Who Whipped a Giant**
Wednesday	**April 18**	**The Woman Who Saved Her Husband's Neck** *1 Samuel 25:1–42*
Thursday	**April 19**	**The Woman Who Saved Her Husband's Neck**
Friday	**April 20**	**The Unknown Who Became Well-Known** *1 Chronicles 4:9–10*
Monday	**April 23**	**The Unknown Who Became Well-Known**

Broadcast schedule is subject to change without notice.

Insight for Living • Post Office Box 69000, Anaheim, CA 92817-0900
Insight for Living Ministries • Post Office Box 2510, Vancouver, BC, Canada V6B 3W7
Insight for Living, Inc. • 20 Albert Street, Blackburn, VIC 3130, Australia

Printed in the United States of America

MEMORABLE SCENES FROM OLD TESTAMENT HOMES

FROM THE BIBLE-TEACHING MINISTRY OF
CHARLES R. SWINDOLL

INSIGHT FOR LIVING

Charles R. Swindoll graduated in 1963 from Dallas Theological Seminary, where he now serves as the school's fourth president, helping to prepare a new generation of men and women for the ministry. Chuck has served in pastorates in three states: Massachusetts, Texas, and California, including almost twenty-three years at the First Evangelical Free Church in Fullerton, California. He is currently senior pastor of Stonebriar Community Church in Frisco, Texas, north of Dallas. His sermon messages have been aired over radio since 1979 as the *Insight for Living* broadcast. A best-selling author, he has written numerous books and booklets on many subjects.

Based on the outlines, charts, and transcripts of Charles. R. Swindoll's sermons, the Bible study guide text was developed and written by Bryce Klabunde, a graduate of Biola University and Dallas Theological Seminary.

Editor in Chief:
Cynthia Swindoll

Study Guide Writer:
Bryce Klabunde

Assistant Editor:
Wendy Peterson

Copy Editors:
Glenda Schlahta
Sue Kimber

Rights and Permissions:
The Meredith Agency

Graphic System Administrator:
Bob Haskins

Director, Communications Division:
John Norton

Print Production Manager:
Don Bernstein

Print Buyer:
Becki Sue Gómez

Unless otherwise identified, all Scripture references are from the New American Standard Bible, © The Lockman Foundation 1960, 1962, 1963, 1968, 1971, 1972, 1973, 1975, 1977, 1995. Used by permission. Scripture taken from the Holy Bible, New International Version, Copyright © 1973, 1978, 1984 International Bible Society, used by permission of Zondervan Bible Publishers [NIV]. Other translations cited are The Living Bible [LB] and the King James Version [KJV].

An effort has been made to locate sources and obtain permission where necessary for the quotations used in this book. In the event of any unintentional omission, a modification will gladly be incorporated in future printings.

ISBN 1-57972-363-2

Cover design: Strata-Media/Robert Page

Cover image: © White/Packert/Image Bank; © Courtney Scott/FPG International LLC; Digital Imagery © Copyright 2001 PhotoDisc, Inc.; Copyright © Kathleen Finlay/Masterfile Corporation 2000

Printed in the United States of America

CONTENTS

INTRODUCTION

Have you ever wished you could have been a bug on the wall of certain homes in the Old Testament? You would be too small to be noticed, but your eyes would be big enough to observe everything. In that unique situation, you could witness all the significant events as they transpired. I've often thought how wonderful that might have been.

Well, this is not a series based on the testimony of bugs on the wall, but rather the reliable witness of the Holy Spirit . . . who was actually there and who led certain people to record what occurred. We'll be transported back into the "time tunnel" and allowed to relive many of those memorable scenes from ancient homes. Our hearts will beat faster as we watch heroism and compassion and quiet trust at their best; and we'll also feel the ache brought on by domestic disharmony, hatred, envy, and even murder. Whatever the emotions we may experience, boredom won't be one of them!

Hopefully, we shall be able to draw out new truths from these old scenes, which time cannot erase. The relevance of God's Word never ceases to amaze me!

Chuck Swindoll

Charles R. Swindoll

PUTTING TRUTH
INTO ACTION

Knowledge apart from application falls short of God's desire for His children. He wants us to apply what we learn so that we will change and grow. This Bible study guide was prepared with these goals in mind. As you go through the following pages, we hope your desire to discover biblical truth will grow as your understanding of God's Word increases and that you will be encouraged to apply what you've learned.

To assist you in your study, we've included a section called Living Insights at the end of each lesson. These exercises will challenge you to study further and to think of specific ways to put your discoveries into action.

There are many ways to use this guide—in personal devotions, group studies, discussions with friends and family, and Sunday School classes. And, of course, it's an ideal study aid when you're listening to its corresponding *Insight for Living* radio series.

To benefit most from this Bible study guide, we would encourage you to consider it a spiritual journal. That's why we've included space in the Living Insights for recording your thoughts and discoveries. We hope you'll return to those sections often for review and encouragement as you continue to grow in your walk with Christ.

Insight for Living

MEMORABLE
SCENES FROM
OLD TESTAMENT
HOMES

Chapter 1

THE SON WHO COULDN'T WIN
Genesis 25:19–34; 26:34–28:9

W hat is it about stories that captivates us and sends our imaginations soaring? It is many things: characters and plot, drama and intrigue, depth and complexity. It is the story's ability to get us involved and make us identify with the people and their situations. And, ultimately, it is the lessons for life that the stories teach us—powerful lessons, timeless, persuasive, and heart-stirring.

All this is true of the great stories of the Old Testament. The apostle Paul recognized the significance of these ancient accounts in Romans 15:4:

> For whatever was written in earlier times was written for our instruction, so that through perseverance and the encouragement of the Scriptures we might have hope.

Carefully rolling out his tattered and worn scrolls, Paul found encouragement and hope in the stories of Israel's past. And that is the goal of our study: to build a reservoir of hope in your life as we peer into a few fascinating scenes played out in the Old Testament. In our first story, the main character is no handsome and virtuous Prince Charming. He is unmistakably human—complete with glaring incapacities, overpowering vices, and hopeless ineptitudes. He is one of the sons of Isaac, a burly lunker of a man named Esau.

Some Observations of a Rejected Son

Esau's story is a tragedy because, in spite of his advantages, he just couldn't win. His life was a doomed voyage in which everything went wrong. Let's look back at Esau's beginnings, stepping aboard to see the leaks and breaches as they occur.

1

His Birth and Childhood

Esau was the fruit of much prayer and patience, for Isaac's wife, Rebekah, was barren for twenty years (see Gen. 25:20–21).[1] However, when Rebekah finally conceived, her joy grew into concern with every month that went by, for she felt a strange struggle in her womb. Esau had a twin brother, and in the secret darkness of Rebekah's womb, they grappled.

> But the children struggled together within her. . . .
> So she went to inquire of the Lord. The Lord said
> to her,
>   "Two nations are in your womb;
>   And two peoples will be separated from
>   your body;
>   And one people will be stronger than the
>   other;
>   And the older shall serve the younger."
> (vv. 22–23)

No sonogram could have told Rebekah what God revealed to her, and no amount of warning could have prepared her for the shock. She and her sixty-year-old husband would parent twins who would be rivals, the younger dominating the older. And this pattern of behavior would carry on for generations. Even the birth itself gave clear evidence of the prophecy.

> When her days to be delivered were fulfilled, behold,
> there were twins in her womb. Now the first came
> forth red, all over like a hairy garment; and they
> named him Esau. Afterward his brother came forth
> with his hand holding on to Esau's heel, so his name
> was called Jacob;[2] and Isaac was sixty years old when
> she gave birth to them. (vv. 24–26)

We are not told much about the boys' childhood, though the wranglings and childish squabbles must have caused a daily fracas.

1. Notice in Genesis 25:20 that "Isaac was forty years old when he took Rebekah . . . to be his wife." But verse 26 tells us that "Isaac was sixty years old when she gave birth to them."

2. *Jacob* comes from a root word meaning "heel," but the implication is to attack someone from behind, "at his heels," and insidiously overtake and supplant that person (see 2 Kings 10:19 and Jer. 17:9, where the root word is also used). William Gesenius, *A Hebrew and English Lexicon of the Old Testament,* trans. Edward Robinson, ed. Francis Brown, S. R. Driver, and Charles A. Briggs (1906; reprint, Oxford, England: Clarendon Press, 1951), pp. 784–85.

No tent was big enough to house these two boys, so Esau found refuge in the fields pursuing his passion for hunting, while Jacob stayed home (v. 27).

Now nothing is disconcerting about the boys' differences in personalities. Even twins can be dissimilar in temperament. But a problem in the family system arose when Isaac and Rebekah played favorites with their sons. Isaac loves Esau—his manly hunter; while Rebekah loved Jacob—her gentle homebody (v. 28). Later in the story, these partialities would play a vital role in the sinking of Esau's ship. But for now, they merely indicate a dry rot that would eventually erode Esau's standing in the family as heir to God's blessing.

His Birthright and Perspective

Being the eldest, Esau had the privilege of the birthright. James Hastings helps us understand what this means.

> To the birthright belonged pre-eminence over the other branches of the family. To the birthright appertained a double portion of the paternal inheritance. To the birthright was attached the land of Canaan, with all its sacred distinctions. To the birthright was given the promise of being the ancestor of the Messiah—the "firstborn among many brethren"—the Saviour in whom all the families of the earth were to be blessed. And to the birthright was added the honour of receiving first, from the mouth of the father, a peculiar benediction, which, proceeding from the spirit of prophecy, was never pronounced in vain. Such were the prospects of Esau.[3]

What bright prospects indeed! No one could stop Esau from enjoying the benefits of first place in the family. No one, that is, except himself. Look at what happens during a seemingly ordinary day over a seemingly ordinary pot of stew.

> And when Jacob had cooked stew, Esau came in from the field and he was famished; and Esau said to Jacob, "Please let me have a swallow of that red stuff there, for I am famished." Therefore his name

---

3. James Hastings, ed., *The Greater Men and Women of the Bible: Adam–Joseph* (Edinburgh, Scotland: T. and T. Clark, 1913), p. 451.

was called Edom. But Jacob said, "First sell me your birthright." And Esau said, "Behold, I am about to die; so of what use then is the birthright to me?" And Jacob said, "First swear to me"; so he swore to him, and sold his birthright to Jacob. Then Jacob gave Esau bread and lentil stew; and he ate and drank, and rose and went on his way. Thus Esau despised his birthright. (vv. 29–34)

What was one's entire future compared to a nice hot bowl of bean soup and bread right out of the oven? Apparently not much, according to Esau. For he saw only his need to fill his empty stomach—his desire for instant gratification. This episode clearly reveals Esau's perspective: future, spiritual priorities were not as important as immediate, physical comforts and pleasures. For this reason even the writer to the Hebrews referred to Esau as a "profane" man (Heb. 12:16 KJV). Cradling his precious bowl of beans, he willingly and defiantly thumbed his nose at his spiritual inheritance and, therefore, blasphemed the Lord (see Num. 15:29–31).

With this one blatant act of blasphemy, Esau's ship stopped dead in the water, while Jacob's glided past to take over first place in the family.

His Struggles and Marriages

Apparently, Isaac was blind to Esau's apathy toward his birthright. And when Esau began hunting for a wife, Isaac again sat quietly, unaware and uninvolved. Though his own father, Abraham, had been a good model of a wise father when he helped Isaac find Rebekah (Gen. 24), this dad gave Esau no such guidance. As a result, Esau brought home not one, but two ungodly, pagan wives (26:34).

Perhaps trying to please his parents by walking in his father's footsteps, Esau married them when he was forty years old—the same age as Isaac when he married Rebekah. But instead of gaining his parents' favor, his foolish marriages resulted in a tense chasm of disappointment between them. In a cryptic, somber tone, Scripture says Esau's wives "brought grief to Isaac and Rebekah" (v. 35).

His Relationships and Reactions

Finally, Esau had one last chance to enter the loop of parental favor. Isaac, believing himself close to death, wanted to honor his heir with the paternal blessing. Let's step into the story and watch the scenes play out. This episode is the climax of Esau's life, the crisis point. Will Esau retake first place? Will he finally show himself to be a winner? The drama builds in four brief scenes.

Scene one. Old, weak, and blind Isaac summons Esau and instructs him to hunt some game and cook it for him. After the meal, Isaac will give him the blessing (27:1–4). Esau jumps at the chance to win back his privileged position, but off to the side, Rebekah is listening.

Scene two. Having overheard the conversation, Rebekah craftily concocts her strategy. Isaac has big plans for "his son," but she will not stand by and let "her son" be overlooked (vv. 5–6, emphasis added). So she hurries to Jacob and says:

> "Go now to the flock and bring me two choice young goats from there, that I may prepare them as a savory dish for your father, such as he loves. Then you shall bring it to your father, that he may eat, so that he may bless you before his death." (vv. 9–10)

Jacob worries that the plan will fail. He is smooth-skinned; surely Isaac will feel him and know he is not Esau. But Rebekah has already thought that through. Wasting no time, she takes the young goats and cooks Isaac's favorite meal. Then she attaches the skins to Jacob's hands and neck, to simulate Esau's hairiness, and clothes him in Esau's finest suit. With the platter of food in his hands, Jacob is ready (vv. 11–17).

Scene three. Jacob enters Isaac's tent. "My father," he says.

The blind man senses something is amiss. "Who are you, my son?"

"I am Esau your firstborn," Jacob replies, doing his best Esau imitation and trying to remember what his mother had told him to say. "I have done as you told me. Get up, please, sit and eat of my game, that you may bless me."

Isaac's brow furrows. "How is it that you have it so quickly, my son?"

Jacob shifts his feet; the platter feels heavy. "Because the Lord your God caused it to happen to me," he says nervously.

Isaac pauses, frozen for a moment. "Please come close," he says, "that I may feel you, my son, whether you are really my son Esau or not."

Trembling, Jacob puts down the platter, straightens the itchy pieces of wool, and approaches. His eyes glance at his father, then drop.

Isaac's wrinkled fingers examine his son. "The voice is the voice of Jacob," he mumbles aloud, "but the hands are the hands of Esau." Looking at Jacob—as a blind man looks, with his ears cocked—Isaac asks, "Are you really my son Esau?"

Jacob slips his hands back. "I am" (see vv. 18–24).

Isaac eats the meal and takes Jacob into his arms. He smells Esau's clothes and is convinced that Jacob is his eldest son. When Isaac bestows the blessing on Jacob, the deception is complete. And Jacob slips away (vv. 25–29).

Scene four. Esau now returns and proudly enters his father's presence with the victuals he has prepared. From behind the tent door, a wail is heard as the two discover the deception. Unable to patch all the ruptures and damage done to his future, all that Esau can do now is receive his father's woeful second blessing (vv. 30–40).

Boiling with rage, Esau vows to take vengeance and kill his brother after his father dies. Rebekah then warns Jacob to flee, but before he leaves, she has one more manipulative tactic to perform. She convinces Isaac that Esau's wives are contemptuous and that Jacob should therefore get a wife from within the family. So Isaac sends Jacob away, thus sparing his life (27:41–28:5).

To close the pitiful episode, Esau makes one last flailing attempt to save his position in the family and keep his sinking ship afloat. Again, it's a foolish choice. Seeing that Jacob's marrying within the family has earned him favor with his father, he decides to follow the same course. But he marries Mahalath, the daughter of Ishmael—Isaac's long-standing rival (vv. 6–9; see also chap. 16)! Esau could not have made a worse decision. Certainly, Esau is the son who couldn't win.

Some Lessons from a Wounded Struggler

What a tragedy. But, as in all tragedies, lessons for life tend to make their way through the smoke and debris.

First: *Instant gratification is a dangerous basis for making a major decision.* Esau's troubles began when he hastily traded his future for a bowl of instant gratification. Don't make that same mistake. Let a major decision sit on the stove and simmer awhile. You may find out that what is in the pot is a brewing batch of poison.

Second: *Parental favoritism has a damaging effect on the whole family.* By preferring one over the other, Isaac and Rebekah did no favors for either son. How easy it is to indulge the likable child and push away the troublesome one. We must seek God's grace so we can learn to love and nurture each of our children equally.

Third: *Unconditional acceptance is a longing in the heart of every child, and no one outgrows it.* Isaac took the time to counsel Jacob concerning a good marriage partner, but his advice was painfully absent with Esau. As a result, Esau's marriages caused his parents much heartache. A disappointment to his father, a failure to his mother, forty-year-old Esau still yearned for his parents' approval. Sadly, scorn and rejection were all he received.

Parents, give your children the unconditional acceptance they long for and need. Take the time to pay attention to their heart-cries. In doing so, you may be the lighthouse your son or daughter needs to avoid life's treacherous rocks and safely navigate life's stormy seas.

 ## Living Insights

It's a trade-off. You give up something to get something. At the office, you give up your time to get money and perks. At home, you give up rest to get a clean house after a day full of messes and spills. Trade-offs are a natural part of life.

But not all trade-offs come easy, and many have disastrous consequences. A case in point: Karen Glance, age 36. She traded her happiness and peace for a $100,000-plus yearly income. "I was a workaholic," she says, "a crazy, crazy woman. I was on a plane four times a week. I just wanted to get to the top. All of a sudden, I realized that I was reaching that goal but I wasn't happy."[4]

Another case: a girl in her teens. Her trade-off included her virginity for a chance at love and security. But she found that "having premarital sex was the worst mistake I ever made. . . . Some day I will marry someone and share something very special with him, but I will also have to tell him of my sickening experience. I dread the day that I have to tell the man I truly love that he is not the only one, though I wish that he was."[5]

---

4. Janice Castro, "The Simple Life," *Time*, April 8, 1991, p. 62.

5. Josh McDowell, *What I Wish My Parents Knew about My Sexuality* (San Bernardino, Calif.: Here's Life Publishers, 1987), p. 218.

Esau's trade-off was his birthright—his future—for a bowl of beans. We say, "How foolish!" And yet many of us have made similar trade-offs that have left us drowning in a sea of regret. Have you made any remorseful trade-offs? Think about them for a minute. What "birthrights" have you traded for a "bowl of beans"?

Birthright	Bowl of Beans

Thinking about the regrettable choices in your past may be difficult. Guilt, sorrow, and pain may seep out of those memories and into your heart. And as you look over the trade-offs you have made through the years, it may even produce a tear or two. Bring those feelings to the Lord.

And consider a final case: a man in his thirties. His trade-off? His life for your tears. "You have sorrow now," Jesus said, "but I will see you again and then you will rejoice; and no one can rob you of that joy" (John 16:22 LB).

 ## Living Insights

At a certain children's hospital, a boy gained a reputation for wreaking havoc with the nurses and staff. One day a visitor who knew about his terrorizing nature made him a deal: "If you are good for a week," she said, "I'll give you a dime when I come again." A week later she stood before his bed. "I'll tell you what," she said, "I won't ask the nurses if you've behaved. You must tell me yourself. Do you deserve the dime?"

After a moment's pause, a small voice from among the sheets said: "Gimme a penny."[6]

We chuckle at the child's creative response because we have known children like that. No matter what incentive they are offered, they cannot behave properly. They are always in trouble,

---

6. *10,000 Jokes, Toasts and Stories,* ed. Lewis and Faye Copeland (Garden City, N.Y.: Garden City Publishing Co., 1940), p. 288.

always messing up, always caught with their hand in every cookie jar imaginable.

Then there is the perfect child. Never says no. Never throws tantrums. Plays quietly. Bestows hugs at just the right moment. And always remembers to feed the dog.

Now be honest. Which child is easier to favor?

Rebekah and Isaac made the mistake of favoring one son over the other, and as a result, the boys' competitive, combative natures were amplified. Each of us has a number of children in our lives—sons, daughters, grandchildren, nephews, nieces, or neighbors. Do you find yourself favoring one child over the other? Do you smile more at one and constantly berate or ignore the other? Think about your attitude as you interact with these children, keeping in mind favoritism's effect on Jacob and Esau. Make it a point to treat each child with the same unconditional acceptance and love.

Chapter 2

THE FARMER WHO MURDERED HIS BROTHER
Genesis 4:1–15

It's hard to put down a good whodunit. Usually the story follows this plot: A wealthy baron is found dead, and the sleuth gets the call. The trail seems impossible to follow, but with one slim lead, he dogs the killer to the last pages of the book. Then, with a dramatic climax, he fingers the culprit and another case is solved.

Murder in real life, though, is far less entertaining.

Almost every day we read about a senseless killing, and we shake our heads in disbelief. Odds are good that murder will even headline tonight's news, which means that right now someone is probably plotting one. That's a chilling thought.

One word aptly describes murder and its effects—tragedy. It's tragic to see the victims, who include not only those killed but also their friends and relatives. And it's tragic to ponder the fate of the killer, whose life is also destroyed. Murder is a tragedy. And tragedies have been with us a long time.

A Brief Survey of Scriptural Tragedies

Paging through the centuries of Scripture, we see the grasping fingers of tragedy reaching through many terrible events besides murder—with God Himself involved in some of them. The Flood killed countless men, women, and children. Thousands fell at Sodom and Gomorrah. God's death plague touched every Egyptian family. And in the wilderness, an entire generation of Hebrews died during forty years of wandering.

Many times, though, people carried out the tragedies, and often those tragedies included murder. Pharaoh and, later, Herod ordered a mass execution of male babies. Moses murdered an Egyptian taskmaster; Joab murdered Absalom; and on and on it goes.

Realizing this murderous rage that foams and ferments within the human heart, God included in the Ten Commandments, "You shall not murder" (Exod. 20:13). He did this because He understood what drives us—our sinful hearts. We sin because we are sinners at heart. We murder because we are murderers at heart. Whether or not we actually kill someone, we all have the capacity to kill when goaded by our sinful inner beast.

That beast emerged early in human history, for it wasn't long after Adam and Eve's rebellion that sin concocted one of its most heinous deeds.

A Careful Study of the First Homicide

In the beginning, Adam and Eve experienced life without sin and its curses. But when they disobeyed God, their innocence was contaminated. And like a river polluted at its source, the entire human race has suffered sin's destructive influences ever since.

In the following scene, we see an immediate effect of Adam and Eve's sin—an effect that pits brother against brother.

The Background

Adam and Eve's family begins, as all do, with the joyful birth of their firstborn, whom they name Cain.[1] Soon they have another son, named Abel,[2] and we know little else about the two boys, except that Cain grows up to become a farmer and Abel a shepherd (Gen. 4:1–2). Eventually, the time comes for the young men to make a sacrifice to the Lord.

> So it came about in the course of time that Cain brought an offering to the Lord of the fruit of the ground. Abel, on his part also brought of the firstlings of his flock and of their fat portions. And the Lord had regard for Abel and for his offering; but for Cain and for his offering He had no regard. (vv. 3–5a)

Why does God reject Cain's offering and accept Abel's? Because Cain has disregarded the acceptable way to approach God, a way both the boys were most likely instructed in by their parents. The principal method to come to God is through an atoning blood

---

1. Eve said, "I have gotten a manchild with the help of the Lord" (Gen. 4:1b). So she named him Cain, qa'yin, which sounds similar to "gotten"—qanah. H. C. Leupold, *Exposition of Genesis* (Grand Rapids, Mich.: Baker Book House, 1942), vol. 1, p. 189.

2. Abel is related to the Hebrew word *hebel* which literally means "vapor, breath." According to one commentary, it may have "indicated generally a feeling of sorrow on account of his weakness, or was a prophetic presentiment of his untimely death." C. F. Keil and F. Delitzsch, *Commentary on the Old Testament* (reprint, Grand Rapids, Mich.: William B. Eerdmans Publishing Co., 1980), vol. 1, p. 109.

sacrifice, as demonstrated throughout the Bible (Heb. 9:22). So, in bringing his agricultural offering, Cain is short-cutting the acceptable path to God. But Abel adheres to God's instructions and brings the best sheep from his flock to be slain. Consequently, God favors Abel's offering but disregards Cain's.

In the New Testament, the writer of Hebrews helps us understand that Abel's obedience was a result of his faith.

> By faith Abel offered to God a better sacrifice than Cain, through which he obtained the testimony that he was righteous, God testifying about his gifts, and through faith, though he is dead, he still speaks. (11:4)

And in his first epistle, John reflects on the root of Cain's unrighteousness.

> For this is the message which you have heard from the beginning, that we should love one another; not as Cain, who was of the evil one and slew his brother. And for what reason did he slay him? Because his deeds were evil, and his brother's were righteous. (3:11–12)

Although Cain may have been sincere, he was unwilling to bring his offering God's way, and as a result, "his deeds were evil." Cain's example warns us that we have to come to God on His terms. He will not conform to our idea of righteousness; we must always conform to His. We may be deeply sincere in our good intentions and good deeds, but if we come to God apart from trusting in the sacrificial blood of Christ, He will have no regard for our efforts.

When God rejects Cain's offering, the sin hidden in Cain's heart surfaces, and he becomes very angry—as the passage says, "his countenance fell" (Gen. 4:5b). Though he does not speak a word, Cain's face plainly betrays his emotions; literally, it says "his face fell." Steaming inside, Cain tightens with rage and pouts like a defiant child. So the Lord, with parental concern, privately pulls him aside for a little talk.

The Warning

> Then the Lord said to Cain, "Why are you angry? And why has your countenance fallen?" (v. 6)

12

Graciously, the Lord prompts Cain to probe his own heart, since He already knows what angers Cain—jealousy. Like a child whose sibling receives a toy or a special privilege, Cain selfishly stamps his feet and sulks. So God advises him,

> "If you do well, will not your countenance be lifted up?" (v. 7a)

"Do right, Cain!" the Lord says. He doesn't say, "Do your best" or "Try real hard." Rather, God reminds him that he is responsible for his own actions, that he can't blame anyone else for his faulty offering, and that he should obey immediately by bringing the proper sacrifice. If he does, his sour-grapes countenance will sweeten. Obedience to God's way uplifts our spirits and gives us inner contentment; disobedience grinds us down so that we feel bitter and hateful.

God warns Cain next about the consequences of his jealous attitude:

> "And if you do not do well, sin is crouching at the door; and its desire is for you, but you must master it." (v. 7b)

Sin is like a sharp-fanged beast with extended claws and tiger-like reactions. It is crouching, waiting, watching. At any moment it may pounce from out of nowhere and devour us. So God says to Cain, "You're vulnerable. The beast is on the loose, but you can master it." Cain can continue through jealousy's doorway, which leads to hatred, murder, and destruction; or he can turn back and obey God, thereby chaining his inner beast. Master or be mastered; the choice is his. The apostle Paul put it this way:

> Be angry, and yet do not sin; do not let the sun go down on your anger, and do not give the devil an opportunity. (Eph. 4:26–27)

We must resolve our anger daily, or we will open the door for the devil. His favorite tools of destruction are the angers and grudges we cling to. And he will use them to dig up resentment, rage, and a desire to kill—if not physically, then emotionally. So we need to work out our anger right away, for then we can control sin's beastly influence.

The Act

Cain hears God's warning, but he doesn't listen. And his jealousy bears bitter fruit:

> Cain told Abel his brother. And it came about when they were in the field, that Cain rose up against Abel his brother and killed him. (Gen. 4:8)

As an act of defiance against God, Cain twists His requirement for an atoning blood sacrifice—shedding righteous Abel's blood instead of a lamb's. "You want a sacrifice, God? How's this!" And Abel falls dead, becoming the first name on history's shamefully long list of murder victims.

We cringe at such a horrible act and think, "I could never do something like that." But if we're honest, many of us would have to confess our own lists of people we've assassinated with our words or attitudes.

The Investigation

Abel's murder takes only a few moments, but after Cain hears his brother's last escaping breath, the haunting silence must seem interminable. It is broken, though, by God's penetrating question:

> "Where is Abel your brother?"[3] (v. 9a)

As He did before, God phrases His question graciously to allow Cain an opportunity to confess. Earlier, Cain just ignored God, but now he responds impudently, "I do not know. Am I my brother's keeper?" (v. 9b).

Sensing no inkling of remorse in Cain, God zeroes in on the facts:

> "What have you done? The voice of your brother's blood is crying to Me from the ground." (v. 10)

Foolishly, Cain thanks he can hide his sin from God. But secret sin on earth is open scandal in heaven. With Abel's blood as Exhibit A, God presents adequate proof to convict Cain of first-degree murder. All that's left is the sentencing.

---

3. Earlier, the Lord questioned Cain's parents in a similar way when they sinned. He said to Adam, "Where are you?" and, "Who told you that you were naked? Have you eaten from the tree of which I commanded you not to eat?" (Gen. 3:9, 11).

The Punishment

Since Abel's blood spilled on the ground, the ground—which was Cain's source of life—would contain the punishment to fit the crime.

> "Now you are cursed from the ground, which has opened its mouth to receive your brother's blood from your hand. When you cultivate the ground, it will no longer yield its strength to you; you will be a vagrant and a wanderer on the earth." (vv. 11–12)

God's words hit Cain like a bucket of cold water, waking him to the severity of his sin. Still, though, his thoughts concern only himself:

> Cain said to the Lord, "My punishment is too great to bear! Behold, You have driven me this day from the face of the ground; and from Your face I will be hidden, and I shall be a vagrant and a wanderer on the earth, and whoever finds me will kill me." (vv. 13–14)

Ironically, the hunter becomes the hunted, and Cain quakes in fear that someone will put a knife in his back.[4] If we were judging him, we'd probably say, "You get what you deserve." But God shows mercy:

> So the Lord said to him, "Therefore whoever kills Cain, vengeance will be taken on him sevenfold." And the Lord appointed a sign for Cain, so that no one finding him would slay him. (v. 15)

Whatever the mark on Cain is, it is not a punishment. It is a protective blessing, for it spares him his brother's bloody fate.

Thus Cain, whose name means "received from the Lord," no longer basks in the Lord's presence. He is forced to wander aimlessly because of the jealousy he allowed to erupt into murder. His story is surely a tragedy.

---

4. Apparently, Cain and Abel were not the only children of Adam and Eve. Cain had a wife (v. 17), who is probably his sister, and those from whom he feared retribution would probably be his other siblings. "He who turned on one of his relatives now must watch out for any of his relatives." Victor P. Hamilton, *The Book of Genesis: Chapters 1–17*, The New International Commentary on the Old Testament, ed. R. K. Harrison (Grand Rapids, Mich.: William B. Eerdmans Publishing Co., 1990), p. 233.

A Personal Search of Our Own Hearts

From Cain's example, we can learn several lessons to help us master sin in our lives.

First: *God's way is the only acceptable way.* There may be a plethora of alternatives to God's way, but all of the them lead to death (compare Prov. 14:12). Only one way leads to life, and the Lord has shown us that way through Jesus Christ. Our part is to believe it and take it.

Second: *Jealousy is a sin that cannot be hidden and must not be tolerated.* If nurtured, jealousy produces resentment, bitterness, and, finally, destruction. Therefore, we must release it if we're to survive.

Third: *When anger is ignored, it never corrects itself.* Some things, like flat tires, demand immediate attention—they just don't fix themselves. The same is true for anger. In fact, if left alone, it will only worsen. So deal with your anger right away, and the first step is to confess it.

Concluding Illustration

One day an eagle swooped to the ground, catching a weasel in its powerful talons. But when it flew away, its wings inexplicably went limp, and it dropped to the ground like a lifeless doll. As it turned out, the weasel had bitten its attacker in midflight, killing the proud eagle as it flew.

If we cling to an attitude of anger or jealousy, it will, like the weasel, sink its teeth into us when we least expect it. We are wise to heed God's words to Cain when sin was at his door: "You must master it." We do that by obediently releasing the sin and soaring again—up to the heights of God's better way.

 ## Living Insights

Jesus said:

> "You have heard that it was said to the people of long ago, 'Do not murder, and anyone who murders will be subject to judgment.' But I tell you that anyone who is angry with his brother will be subject to judgment. Again, anyone who says to his brother, 'Raca,' is answerable to the Sanhedrin. But anyone

who says, 'You fool!' will be in danger of the fire of hell." (Matt. 5:21–22 NIV)

In Jesus' world of jurisprudence, one is guilty of murder long before the threatening words and the smoking gun. According to Jesus, even unspoken anger is worthy of the verdict "Guilty."

If you were standing in court before Jesus, how would you plead if you were accused of hidden anger toward someone you know?

❐ Guilty   ❐ Innocent

If you pled guilty, who are you angry with? Why are you angry?

_____

_____

_____

Like smoldering embers, feelings of anger are difficult to conceal. Eventually, someone will smell something burning or see the smoke. Has the smoke from your anger been coming out in your words or your attitudes? If so, in what ways?

_____

_____

_____

_____

Admitting your anger and recognizing its damaging effects on others is the first step toward pouring water on its flames. In the next Living Insight, we'll look at ways to douse your anger entirely.

 Living Insights   STUDY ONE

If the heart is anger's hotbed, then the tongue is anger's flame. That's why words like "raca"—a derogatory term equivalent to "airhead"—or "you fool" or other more subtle burns are so serious. According to Jesus, these words reveal a heart that is white-hot with anger, and He says that the one who speaks them is as guilty as a murderer.

If anger is that deadly, we must let go of it. But how? Frank

17

Minirth and Paul Meier give a few helpful suggestions:

- Acknowledge that bitterness is futile, and choose to put it aside.

- Express your anger appropriately, instead of trying to hold it in.

- Speak positively to and about anyone who has hurt you.

- Develop self-control.

- Choose to forgive when wronged.[5]

Let's go through these suggestions one at a time. First, acknowledge the futility of your bitterness right now and express your commitment to release your anger.

_____

_____

How can you communicate your feelings to the person with whom you are angry? Write down the words you would choose.

I feel _____

_____

Next, turn around your negativity toward that person. What positive attributes does that person have?

_____

_____

Emotions can sometimes feel out of control. You can gain control by yielding your thoughts to Christ. Meditate on Philippians 4:4–9, and commit yourself to depending on Him when angry thoughts attack again.

Finally, let an attitude of forgiveness extinguish any remaining anger in your heart. Write out your words of forgiveness to the person who has injured you.

_____

_____

5. Frank B. Minirth and Paul D. Meier, with Kevin Kinback, *Ask the Doctors* (Grand Rapids, Mich.: Baker Book House, 1991), p. 31.

Chapter 3

THE PATRIARCH WHO LOST IT ALL

Job 1–2; 42:7–17

Take a drive through an average American suburb. What do you see? You might notice a natural canopy of evenly spaced trees, leaf-littered lawns for cartwheels or touch football, shingled roofs for stormy-night security, and bay windows for early morning bird watching.

But that is just on the outside. If you know the street, you recognize the people, like little Stacey. Her oldest brother left home last year, and her parents still don't know where he is. Like Mr. Crenshaw. He lost his job ten months ago. Like the Martins' boy. He's been in the hospital for weeks. Or like the Clifton family. George is an alcoholic.

Broken hearts are all around us, in the house next door, in the adjoining cubicle at work, and in the seat beside us at church. In fact, pain is one of the few things we all have in common. Maybe you're the one with the crushed spirit right now—the hidden heartache that is too deep for words and too private for prayer chains. Unfortunately, no easy, three-step method exists for erasing pain. We can dissect it, describe it, and analyze it, but we can't make it go away. We can, however, learn to face it. And that is the value of this story, which took place just down the block and to the right—in Job's house.

Job's Character and First Series of Tests

Most people know about Job. His name has been synonymous with the word *patience* since at least the first century,[1] and his endurance through a cornucopia of disasters amazes us even today. But do we really *know* Job?

What Kind of Man Was He?

Aside from his patience, what was Job's character really like? We must begin with this question, because his character is the element

---

1. The age-old saying "the patience of Job" has its origin in James' epistle (see James 5:11 KJV).

of the story that defies our nice, neat platitudes. It seems fair that tragedy should strike the cruel and wicked. But Job was "blameless, upright, fearing God and turning away from evil" (Job 1:1). He headed a large and loving family (vv. 2, 4), managed a prosperous business (v. 3), and regularly worshiped the Lord (v. 5). He was even considered "the greatest of all the men of the east" (v. 3b).

Because of his integrity and heart for God, we would think that Job should have enjoyed a long life of blessings and honors. Yet he received the opposite: the whip of suffering.

What Kind of Calamities Struck Him?

Job's sufferings were prompted by an interchange between Satan and God. When Satan presented himself to the Lord along with the "sons of God" (v. 6),[2] Job became the topic of their conversation:

> The Lord said to Satan, "Have you considered My servant Job? For there is no one like him on the earth, a blameless and upright man, fearing God and turning away from evil." (v. 8)

But Satan hissed:

> "Does Job fear God for nothing? Have You not made a hedge about him and his house and all that he has, on every side? You have blessed the work of his hands, and his possessions have increased in the land. But put forth Your hand now and touch all that he has; he will surely curse You to Your face." Then the Lord said to Satan, "Behold, all that he has is in your power, only do not put forth your hand on him." So Satan departed from the presence of the Lord. (vv. 9–12)

Wasting no time, Satan began his diabolical onslaught. He sent the Sabeans to slaughter Job's oxen, donkeys, and servants (vv. 13–15); he issued fire from heaven to incinerate Job's sheep and shepherds (v. 16); and he incited the Chaldeans to steal Job's camels and murder more servants (v. 17). Then, rearing back for

---

2. The "sons of God" are angels. "Unfallen angels are God's 'sons' in the sense that they are His creation; cf. 38:7." Roy B. Zuck, "Job," *The Bible Knowledge Commentary*, Old Testament volume, ed. John F. Walvoord and Roy B. Zuck (Wheaton, Ill.: SP Publications, Victor Books, 1985), p. 719.

his final punch, he raised a ferocious wind to blow down the house where Job's children were gathered. All were killed instantly (vv. 18–19).

Terrible, tragic events. And what makes them even more terrible is the speed with which they occurred. For just as one messenger had reported a calamity, another came to tell of a new horror— "While he was still speaking, another also came and said . . ." (vv. 16, 17, 18). Within minutes and without warning, four horrific tragedies knocked Job reeling.

Job's Response and Second Major Test

Imagine such tragedies crashing in on you all at once. The heartache would feel unbearable, and even the strongest might despair and doubt God's love. But how does Job respond?

Reaction to Affliction

> Then Job arose and tore his robe and shaved his head, and he fell to the ground and worshiped. He said,
> "Naked I came from my mother's womb,
> And naked I shall return there.
> The Lord gave and the Lord has taken away.
> Blessed be the name of the Lord."
> Through all this Job did not sin nor did he blame God. (vv. 20–22)

No cynicism, no blame, no doubt. How can Job respond with such faith? Because of the healthy condition of his soul. He knows that the Lord is the sovereign of his life, and that He who has blessed him has every right to also allow suffering. And when it is well with your soul, the blast of pain's furnace is not quite so hot.

The Consummate Loss

Job has passed the first fiery test, but Satan has another cruel plan in mind. This time, he wants to inflict the consummate loss— the loss of health. So with wicked delight, he comes before God again and says:

> "Skin for skin! Yes, all that a man has he will give for his life. However, put forth Your hand, now, and touch his bone and his flesh; he will curse You to

Your face." So the Lord said to Satan, "Behold, he is in your power, only spare his life." (2:4b–6)

"Only spare his life," God says. Our adversary operates under tight controls—never think of him as omnipotent. He is a defeated foe, scrambling for whatever ground he can get.

With Job now at his mercy, Satan charges to accomplish his scheme.

> Then Satan went out from the presence of the Lord and smote Job with sore boils from the sole of his foot to the crown of his head. And he took a potsherd to scrape himself while he was sitting among the ashes. (vv. 7–8)

One commentator describes Job's affliction as

> *elephantiasis* (so called because the limbs become jointless lumps like elephants' legs). . . . The disease begins with the rising of tubercular boils, and at length resembles a cancer spreading itself over the whole body, by which the body is so affected, that some of the limbs fall completely away. Scraping with a potsherd will not only relieve the intolerable itching of the skin, but also remove the matter.[3]

Such suffering staggers the imagination! And what compounds Job's agony is that there is no apparent reason for it. Remember, he is a blameless and upright man who fears God, turns away from evil, and faithfully intercedes for his family (1:1, 5). He has done nothing to deserve these tragedies.

A tormented and wretched sight, Job sits in agony with only one remaining source of comfort since the loss of his children—his wife. But the ten fresh graves are also calling out to her. And in her own grief and rage, her heart ravaged by the sight of her pitiful husband, she explodes with a torrent of desperate, excruciating words:

> "Do you still hold fast your integrity? Curse God and die!" (2:9)

3. C. F. Keil and F. Delitzsch, *Commentary on the Old Testament* (reprint, Grand Rapids, Mich.: William B. Eerdmans Publishing Co., 1978), vol. 4, pp. 69–70.

Will Job give in to her counsel? How intense the temptation must have been! But again he demonstrates the depth of his character as he turns and speaks to his distraught wife:

> "You speak as one of the foolish women speaks. Shall we indeed accept good from God and not accept adversity?" (v. 10a)

Job's theology allows for suffering—even for the righteous. Some modern teachers say that God only gives good and adversity is a sign of our lack of faith. Job knows, however, that God is sovereign and allows raging storms or pleasant breezes according to His will. And although it must have been torturous for Job not to understand all the reasons behind God's will, he was able to trust the Lord in both good times and bad. As a result, "In all this Job did not sin with his lips" (v. 10b). All Satan's attempts to provoke this righteous man to curse his God came to nothing because Job stayed faithful in word and deed.

Job's "Friends" and Ultimate Triumph

Job's story is not over, however. In fact, it has only begun, for he must endure even more mental anguish from his insensitive friends.

His So-Called Counselors

Job's wife is not the only well-meaning counselor who offers him bad advice. His friends Eliphaz, Bildad, and Zophar also come to his side (vv. 11–13). And through most of the rest of the book, they wrangle back and forth with him, doing more finger-pointing than consoling and more preaching than showing mercy. They try to do what no person can do for another, which is to declare dogmatically why someone is suffering. It would have been far better for them to have left that issue with God.

God's Gracious Rewards

When all has been said, God Himself takes the microphone. First, He sternly addresses Job's unwise counselors:

> The Lord said to Eliphaz the Temanite, "My wrath is kindled against you and against your two friends, because you have not spoken of Me what is right as My servant Job has." (42:7)

When we accept the role of counselor, we take on an awesome responsibility. People entrust their sorrows, their questions, their hearts to us, and we minister to them by showing them God's tender heart. This should never be done glibly or without careful thought, for it matters very much to God that we speak "what is right" of Him. After Job's friends repent and he intercedes for them (vv. 8–9), God reaches down and touches his life, not with the ruinous hand of Satan but with a restorative touch of blessing.

> The Lord restored the fortunes of Job when he prayed for his friends, and the Lord increased all that Job had twofold. . . . The Lord blessed the latter days of Job more than his beginning, and he had 14,000 sheep and 6,000 camels and 1,000 yoke of oxen and 1,000 female donkeys. He had seven sons and three daughters. . . . After this, Job lived 140 years, and saw his sons and his grandsons, four generations. And Job died, an old man and full of days. (vv. 10, 12–13, 16–17)

Several Reasons Bad Things Happen to God's People

Blessed, broken, and blessed again, Job probably never fully understood why he had to endure the jolting pain God allowed to overwhelm his life. In our walk through life, we may encounter similar blows, leaving us shaking our heads and wondering why such bad things happen to God's people. But from Job's example and the Bible in general, we can formulate some partial answers to this question.

To develop faith. Suffering produces dependence on the Lord because it takes us beyond self-sufficiency. We have no other recourse than to rely on Him, and that develops a stronger faith (see 1 Pet. 5:8–10).

To reveal true character. As Moses told the Hebrews who had wandered in the desert for forty long, painful years, "The Lord your God has led you in the wilderness . . . that He might humble you, testing you, to know what was in your heart" (Deut. 8:2). Even Job realized this aspect of pain, saying, "But He knows the way I take; When He has tried me, I shall come forth as gold" (Job 23:10). Suffering reveals what is in our hearts, the true nature of our character.

To expose hidden or hurtful sin. Pain is a purifier. It causes us to examine ourselves closely to see if there are any unconfessed sins hidden in the corners of our hearts. During times of pain, it is wise to pray as David prayed,

> Search me, O God, and know my heart;
> Try me and know my anxious thoughts;
> And see if there be any hurtful way in me,
> And lead me in the everlasting way.
> (Ps. 139:23–24)

To learn obedience. Suffering also trains us to obey God. Hebrews 5:8 says, "[Jesus] learned obedience from the things which He suffered." Trials make difficult schoolmasters, but the result will be a closer and more obedient walk with the Lord.

To keep down pride. Paul learned that his painful "thorn in the flesh" served a vital role in keeping him humble (2 Cor. 12:7). Suffering has a way of reminding us of our limitations, keeping us aware of our dependence on God.

To glorify God. The light at the end of pain's tunnel is the promise that through our suffering, our faith will grow and God will be glorified. "In this you greatly rejoice," Peter wrote,

> even though now for a little while, if necessary, you have been distressed by various trials, so that the proof of your faith, being more precious than gold which is perishable, even though tested by fire, may be found to result in praise and glory and honor at the revelation of Jesus Christ. (1 Pet. 1:6–7)

Reading about suffering is one thing; coping with it is entirely different. If you're the one on Job's ash heap today, desperately needing relief, you may find that the best answer to the why question is not a reason but a Person.

> Sixteen times Job had hurled to the heavens his anguished question, "Why?" But God never answered the question *why.*
>
> Fifty-nine times we encounter the word "who" in reference to God. And that simple change of a "y" to an "o" is what made all the difference. . . .
>
> Job did not need to know why. He just needed to know who—who was in control; who cared for him; who would sustain and vindicate him.[4]

4. Henry Gariepy, *Portraits of Perseverance* (Wheaton, Ill.: Scripture Press Publications, Victor Books, 1989), pp. 205–6.

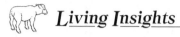

On the one hand, Job's is the story of "The Patriarch Who Lost It All"; but on the other hand, his is the story of "The Patriarch Who Lost All *but Faith.*"

> For Job did not lose everything. He held onto that which is most precious—that which the most severe loss and suffering, and even death, cannot destroy or take from us. For the story of Job is the story of a man who kept his faith in spite of the worst misfortunes, in spite of his world tumbling down around him, in spite of crushing heartbreak.[5]

However perilously close to the Grand Canyon edge of doubt and despair Job came, he remained faithful to the Lord. That is why Satan failed to destroy Job completely, and that is what gives us hope when suffering pushes us to the edge.

How close have you come to the edge of despair? Write of your own experience, past or present, when suffering pushed you close to doubting the Lord.

_____

_____

_____

_____

_____

At times like these, is there any way we can hold on to God in faith, when it is He whom we question?

Job teaches us how. "I have heard of You," he says to God, "by the hearing of the ear; But now my eye *sees* You" (Job 42:5, emphasis added). You may have heard of God from others, but now, in your suffering, you must see Him yourself.

What do you see when you look at God? Do you see Jesus? Do you see Him weeping with you in your pain? Do you see Him suffering for you on the cross? Do you see Him rising from the grave,

---

5. Gariepy, *Portraits of Perseverance*, p. 63.

motioning for you to one day follow? Write what you see. And in
faith, step back from the edge into the arms of your Savior, who
welcomes you in your suffering.

I see a God who _____

_____

_____

_____

_____

_____

_____

Living Insights STUDY TWO

Suffering, like being born, is a process that connects us to a
richer, unforeseen reality. Once the way is entered, we move slowly,
painfully to the light. But in spite of the intensity of our passage,
the unalterable fact and promise is that we do move.

> "To suffer passes; to have suffered never passes." The
> pain will one day cease. But what we learn in the
> time of trial is our treasure forever. Misfortune never
> leaves us where it finds us.[6]

The six reasons for suffering that we discussed in the lesson are
the ways that pain begets a deeper richness in our Christian life.
Consider your own sufferings and describe what they have taught
you in each of the following areas.

Faith _____

_____

_____

Character _____

6. Gariepy, *Portraits of Perseverance*, p. 211.

_____

_____

Sin _____

_____

_____

Obedience _____

_____

_____

Pride _____

_____

_____

Glorifying God _____

_____

_____

Chapter 4

THE FATHER WHO RELEASED HIS SON

Genesis 22:1–14

> I've learned that we must hold everything loosely,
> because when I grip it tightly, it hurts when the
> Father pries my fingers loose and takes it from me.
>
> Corrie ten Boom[1]

White-knuckled and weary, sometimes we hold things in life so tightly that we focus on little else than maintaining our iron grip. Even the *thought* of losing these things sends flashes of panic through our soul. And we grit our teeth, determined to clutch them even tighter, never . . . letting . . . go!

It is at these times that our loving Father must pry our fingers loose and remove what has so preoccupied us. "But," we protest, "doesn't He know how much we need these things? Can't He see that our position, our future, our *lives* depend on them?"

When our hands are finally empty and the pain of letting go has passed, however, a subtle realization settles on our soul—God is all we really need.

And the test is over.

This kind of faith-building test is the subject of today's scene from the Old Testament. In order to enter more fully into this story, we first need to face the areas in which we struggle to hold things loosely.

Releasing Things Valuable

We can fit the things we have difficulty releasing into four categories.

Our possessions. With one fateful flash of lightning, a houseful of treasures burns to the ground. A tornado rips through your town and everything you own is strewn across the neighborhood. These kinds of disasters may never touch you, but how would you respond if they did? It is important, now, to relax your hold on your possessions.

---

1. In a private conversation between Corrie ten Boom and Chuck Swindoll.

Our occupations. Pink slips land on desks every day, and thousands of men and women lose their jobs—sometimes without warning. So don't allow your self-image to be tied to your work, because your job can change in an instant. Don't let your career or your spouse's become a god. Hold it loosely.

Our plans and dreams. Cherished dreams keep us motivated and alive with hope. Starting a new business, completing your education, marriage, children, retirement, travel—these are all exciting adventures. But hold them loosely, for sometimes dreams can die.

Our relationships. Who does not fear losing a child, a parent, a spouse, a dear friend? Circumstances may move them miles away, or death's indiscriminate finger may touch them. Good-byes will always be a part of our lives. So love people deeply, but remember, when it's time, let them go.

Faith to release those people dearest to us is the heart of today's story. It is a bittersweet account that begins with God's disquieting instructions to a father named Abraham to release his precious treasure—Isaac, his son.

When a Father Released His Son

Of all the father-son stories in Scripture, none pulls at our heartstrings more than this one. Abraham, who is now over one hundred years old and who had had little hope even to have Isaac because of his age and the age of his wife (see Gen. 18:9–15; 21:5), is told by God to sacrifice his son.

A Command to Be Obeyed

Without warning, this lightning-bolt command streaks across Abraham's heart.

> Now it came about after these things, that God tested[2] Abraham, and said to him, "Abraham!" And he said, "Here I am." He said, "Take now your son, your only son, whom you love, Isaac, and go to the land of Moriah, and offer him there as a burnt

---

2. The word "tested" in verse 1 is in a grammatical form called the *piel stem,* which intensifies the verb's action. It is actually saying that God intensely tested Abraham—that this was to be a test like no other.

offering[3] on one of the mountains of which I will tell you." (22:1–2)

Why would a God who is kind and gentle and loving even *ask* such a thing of this man—or of any father? God had never before, nor has He since, asked for a human sacrifice. Why now? Why Isaac?

God made this request for two reasons. The first was to test the authenticity and depth of Abraham's faith. The second was to remind Abraham that we are to adore God as the Giver of gifts even more than we adore the gifts He gives. How often we want to worship the "Isaacs" He has put in our lives! But God wants us to have the security that comes only from anchoring ourselves on His unfailing love and not tying our hope to temporal relationships.

Swift and Complete Obedience

How will Abraham respond to God's test? Will he argue? Will he vacillate? Will he try to bargain with God? Let's read on to find out.

So Abraham rose early in the morning and saddled his donkey, and took two of his young men with him and Isaac his son; and he split wood for the burnt offering, and arose and went to the place of which God had told him. On the third day Abraham raised his eyes and saw the place from a distance. Abraham said to his young men, "Stay here with the donkey, and I and the lad will go over there, and we will worship and return to you." (vv. 3–5)

No whining. No pleading. No stubborn refusal. Just acceptance and trust. Three things are remarkable about Abraham's response. First, *the speed with which he obeys*. Without hesitancy or questioning, he sets off to do God's will. Second, *the simplicity of his faith*. Did you catch his words to his servants? "*We* will worship and return to you" (emphasis added). How can Abraham think that Isaac will return if he is to be sacrificed? Because Abraham knows that God will somehow allow them to walk back down that mountain

---

3. The Hebrew word used here for "offering," *'olah*, refers to a whole burnt offering, which would have included an animal's hooves, face, head, skin—everything. The entire animal would be consumed in smoke, and this is just what God has told Abraham to do with Isaac. Commentator H. C. Leupold adds that "it typifies complete surrender to God. . . . The son given to Abraham is to be given back to Yahweh without reservations of any sort." *Exposition of Genesis* (Grand Rapids, Mich.: Baker Book House, 1942), vol. 2, p. 621.

together—even if it means resurrecting Isaac from the dead (see Heb. 11:17–19).[4]

So, believing that God "causes all things to work together for good" (Rom. 8:28), Abraham commends himself and Isaac into the Lord's hands:

> Abraham took the wood of the burnt offering and laid it on Isaac his son, and he took in his hand the fire and the knife. So the two of them walked on together. (Gen. 22:6)

But then Isaac, who is probably a young man at the time of this story, takes a quick inventory—wood, check; fire, check; knife, check; offering . . . offering! He turns to his father and says,

> "Behold, the fire and the wood, but where is the lamb for the burnt offering?" (v. 7b)

The old man pauses. *His* faith is being tested, not his son's. How can he burden his son with the whole truth? Yet he cannot lie. Instead, he simply expresses his faith in God:

> "God will provide for Himself the lamb for the burnt offering, my son." So the two of them walked on together. (v. 8)

Together they walk; together they trust the Lord. Side by side, a father and a son climb the perilous heights of God's will. When they arrive at the "place of which God had told him" (v. 9a), Abraham builds an altar and Isaac stands by, silently watching.

At this point, we see the third remarkable thing about Abraham's response—*the thoroughness of his obedience*. Every detail of his actions reveals his resolve to carry out God's command.

> And Abraham built the altar there and arranged the wood, and bound his son Isaac and laid him on the altar, on top of the wood. (v. 9b)

Abraham doesn't say, "OK, Isaac, let's put on a good show, let's just pretend that we're going through with this sacrifice. I'll use this phony knife, you squirm a little, and . . ." No, Abraham uses real

---

4. Abraham's confidence was based upon God's promise to him that he would be "the father of a multitude of nations" (Gen. 17:5).

rope, real wood, and a real knife—risking Isaac's life and his own future in obedience to God.

Unlike Abraham, we often avoid risk, being unwilling to surrender our lives to God 100 percent. But without risk, we lose the key that unlocks the abundant life God wants to give us. Eileen Guder illustrates this point well:

> You can live on bland food so as to avoid an ulcer; drink no tea or coffee or other stimulants, in the name of health; go to bed early and stay away from night life; avoid all controversial subjects so as never to give offense; mind your own business and avoid involvement in other people's problems; spend money only on necessities and save all you can. You can still break your neck in the bathtub, and it will serve you right.[5]

It certainly can't be said of Abraham and Isaac that they did not take chances in obeying the Lord. For when the stones were in place and the wood piled high, Abraham "stretched out his hand, and took the knife to slay his son" (v. 10).

The moment had come. The shocking command of the Lord, the three-day journey, the mental anguish, the emotional walk up the hill. And now with one quick motion it would be over—Isaac would be dead.

Relief and Reward

"Abraham, Abraham!" The voice of the angel of the Lord bursts from the sky (v. 11a).[6] Imagine Abraham's relief as he hoarsely calls back, "Here I am" (v. 11b). And the next words are a soft, cool shower from heaven:

> "Do not stretch out your hand against the lad, and do nothing to him; for now I know that you fear God, since you have not withheld your son, your only son, from Me." (v. 12)

---

5. Eileen Guder, God, But I'm Bored, as quoted by Tim Hansel in Holy Sweat (Waco, Tex.: Word Books, 1987), p. 48.

6. In Hebrew, a name is repeated out of respect. It's as if God were saying, "I need no more proof; you have validated your faith, Abraham."

Drenched in the joy these words bring, Abraham drops his knife and helps Isaac off the altar, holding his son close to him. The test is over.

But God is not through.

> Then Abraham raised his eyes and looked, and behold, behind him a ram caught in the thicket by his horns; and Abraham went and took the ram and offered him up for a burnt offering in the place of his son. Abraham called the name of that place The Lord Will Provide, as it is said to this day, "In the mount of the Lord it will be provided." (vv. 13–14)

Using that same rope and that same altar, Abraham sacrifices the ram . . . instead of Isaac.

Analogies Worth Pondering

Mount Moriah. Here a father released his son.

Centuries later, after kingdoms had come and gone, after timeless sands had covered Abraham's and Isaac's footprints, this mountain came to be known by another name—Calvary. And here another Father released His Son. Let's take a moment to ponder the similarities between Abraham and Isaac, God and Christ.

God the Father showed us how to give when He released His dear Son to us . . . at Bethlehem. As Abraham let go of his son, so also the Father gave us His only Son on that first Christmas—really, nine months earlier, as He allowed Jesus to become a tiny embryo in Mary's womb. Then, when He was born, He became a helpless, crying infant who would grow and play and learn . . . and suffer for our sins.

God the Son showed us how to die when He released Himself to the Father . . . at Calvary. As Isaac submitted himself to his father without fighting and in quiet trust, so Jesus offered Himself to the Father, praying, "Yet not My will, but Yours be done" (Luke 22:42b).

God the Holy Spirit will show us how to live when we release whatever has us in its grip . . . through obedience. Abraham passed the test because he released Isaac. What is it that God desires you to hold more loosely, maybe release entirely? A possession? An occupation? A dream? A person? With the power of the Holy Spirit, you can let go.

As you do, let A. W. Tozer's prayer become your own.

Father, I want to know Thee, but my coward heart fears to give up its toys. I cannot part with them without inward bleeding, and I do not try to hide from Thee the terror of the parting. I come trembling, but I do come. Please root from my heart all those things which I have cherished so long and which have become a very part of my living self, so that Thou mayest enter and dwell there without a rival. Then shalt Thou make the place of Thy feet glorious. Then shall my heart have no need of the sun to shine in it, for Thyself wilt be the light of it, and there shall be no night there. In Jesus' Name, Amen.[7]

 ## Living Insights

Every parent who has choked back a tear on a child's first day of school understands releasing. Every retiree who tapes the last box, removes the last picture, and says the last good-bye understands releasing. Any who have felt money and possessions slip through their fingers, any who have waved at a disappearing moving van, any who have taken a heart-wrenching walk past a coffin understand releasing too.

Maybe you identify with some of these situations. In the space provided, describe a time when you had to release something or someone you dearly loved. What were the circumstances? How did you feel?

_____

_____

_____

_____

_____

From your experience, you understand releasing as well. But maybe for you the releasing process felt a little like robbery. Your

7. A. W. Tozer, *The Pursuit of God* (Harrisburg, Pa.: Christian Publications, 1948), p. 31.

treasure was suddenly wrenched from your hands, and you still mourn its loss.

If the pain of that loss still haunts you, maybe you have not really released it. You are still clinging, even though it—or they—are gone.

But the Giver, in His providence, has removed the gift. In its place, He wants to give you a richer treasure—Himself. Will you cling to Him alone?

> One by one He took them from me,
> All the things I valued most,
> Until I was empty-handed;
> Every glittering toy was lost,
>
> And I walked earth's highways, grieving,
> In my rags and poverty.
> Till I heard His voice inviting,
> "Lift your empty hands to Me!"
>
> So I held my hands toward Heaven,
> And He filled them with a store
> Of His own transcendent riches
> Till they could contain no more.
>
> And at last I comprehended
> With my stupid mind and dull,
> That God COULD not pour His riches
> Into hands already full![8]

 Living Insights

No child can resist a balance-testing walk along the top of a brick wall. With arms stretched out like wings and tongue stuck to the upper lip, the child gingerly teeters across the wall that was, after all, put there for this very purpose.

Now imagine this tightrope wall-walking act was being done by your son or daughter! Would you pull him off right away? Would you hold her hand? Stand within catching distance? Watch anxiously from afar?

---

8. Martha Snell Nicholson, "Treasures," in *Ivory Palaces* (Wilmington, Calif.: Martha Snell Nicholson, 1946), p. 67.

Eventually, your children will outgrow walking on walls, but their desire to test their skills, forge ahead on their own, and become a man or a woman will never diminish. Will you be able to release them?

If you have children, in what ways are they expressing their independence and self-sufficiency?

_____

_____

_____

_____

_____

Abraham had to release his son, Isaac, into the hands of God. How can you begin releasing *your* child to God?

_____

_____

_____

_____

_____

As your children grow, God will ask you to release them more and more. Commit yourself to letting them go when the time is right. They may fall once or twice, but they will learn. Then you can applaud.

Chapter 5

THE BOY WHO HEARD GOD'S VOICE

1 Samuel 3:1–18

Every month, *Life* magazine features a story on the last page of the issue. What makes the story unique is that few, if any, words are used. A *photograph* tells the story. Within this one eloquent scene, we see characters interacting and a plot unfolding; we see life caught in action.

The photograph may tell a story that involves suspense, romance, or humor; and if the picture is just right, it portrays the central climax of the story, the crisis. And if we enter into the lives of the characters, we can sometimes foresee a resolution. The photograph story has reached out and caught us, and we savor the feelings it brings.

Still Frames . . . Significant Events

Can all that really be captured in a single picture? Yes, and many times a picture can relate a story more succinctly and with greater impact than words. Recall, for example, the pictures of Bible characters used by your childhood Sunday school teacher. One of those pictures showed a little girl standing in the bulrushes, watching a princess open a wicker basket with baby Moses inside. Another showed storm clouds, high waves, and a boxy boat with a giraffe's head poking through a window.

As we thumb through the stack, one picture stands out. It's not David hurling his stone at Goliath. It's not Daniel bravely facing the hungry lions. It's a small boy in a nightdress in a room dimly lit by a single lamp. The boy gazes up to the ceiling, clutching his bed covers. His face tells the story—for it is frightened, yet curious; unsure, yet willing. And on his innocent lips you can almost hear the words, "Speak, for Your servant is listening" (1 Sam. 3:10).

God's Voice . . . Samuel's Response

This young boy's story occurs at a time in Israel's history when things have become dull. Without the excitement of war or political intrigue, the nation is experiencing a rare period of waveless calm. And onto that smooth-as-glass sea God drops a tiny pebble named Samuel. In the years ahead, the ripples of his life will multiply and spread, rocking an entire nation. But for now the water is still, and Samuel is just a boy.

> Now the boy Samuel was ministering to the Lord before Eli. And word from the Lord was rare in those days, visions were infrequent. (v. 1)

Samuel's mother has taken him to live with Eli, the aging high priest.[1] His life consists of helping the priests of the tabernacle at Shiloh, which is his new home. One night, an amazing thing happens . . .

> It happened at that time as Eli was lying down in his place (now his eyesight had begun to grow dim and he could not see well), and the lamp of God had not yet gone out, and Samuel was lying down in the temple of the Lord where the ark of God was, that the Lord called Samuel; and he said, "Here I am." (vv. 2–4)

Samuel mistakes God's voice for Eli's; jumping to obey his master, he enters the old man's chamber.

> Then he ran to Eli and said, "Here I am, for you called me." But he said, "I did not call, lie down again." So he went and lay down. The Lord called yet again, "Samuel!" So Samuel arose and went to Eli and said, "Here I am, for you called me." But he answered, "I did not call, my son, lie down again." (vv. 5–6)

Twice Samuel hears a voice, and twice he scampers to Eli. The two of them are perplexed. Samuel has been so stable and trustworthy; can he be hearing things? Or is Eli becoming senile, calling in his sleep without knowing it? Could Hophni or Phinehas, Eli's two profligate sons, be behind this humorless joke? Samuel retraces his steps to bed, confused and a little frightened.

---

1. Hannah, Samuel's mother, prayed to the Lord to give her a son. She promised God that if He would grant her request, she would dedicate him to the Lord for lifetime service in the temple. So when Samuel was born and weaned, she presented him to Eli the high priest (1 Sam. 1:1–28).

It does not occur to Samuel that it may be the Lord who is calling him. He has never heard God's voice before. So when God calls, "Samuel!" a third time, for the third time Samuel enters Eli's chamber. This time Samuel is sure. A voice did call his name; it was real and he heard it (vv. 7–8a).

Though his eyes were dim, Eli's spirit could see that this was no ordinary event. So, giving speechless Samuel the words to say—what do you say when God talks to you?—he sends Samuel back to his bedchamber, an unlikely Holy of Holies.

> Then Eli discerned that the Lord was calling the boy. And Eli said to Samuel, "Go lie down, and it shall be if He calls you, that you shall say, 'Speak, Lord, for Your servant is listening.'" So Samuel went and lay down in his place.
>
> Then the Lord came and stood and called as at other times, "Samuel! Samuel!" And Samuel said, "Speak, for Your servant is listening." (vv. 8b–10)

At this point, most Sunday school teachers remove their spectacles, close their picture books, and begin moralizing. But the story is only half told. The questions have not been answered. What is God's message to Samuel? And what will this message mean for Eli and his sons and for the life of Israel?

God's Warning . . . Samuel's Reluctance

In the quietness of Samuel's bedchamber, God reveals to this young prophet the first of many grim messages that will come to him through his years as God's man of the hour. The message is based on a previous prophecy that was given to Eli by an unknown "man of God," and it is important to review the nature of that prediction.

> Then a man of God came to Eli and said to him, "Thus says the Lord, . . . 'Why do you kick at My sacrifice and at My offering which I have commanded in My dwelling, and honor your sons above Me, by making yourselves fat with the choicest of every offering of My people Israel?' Therefore the Lord God of Israel declares, 'I did indeed say that your house and the house of your father should walk before Me forever'; but now the Lord declares, 'Far

be it from Me—for those who honor Me I will honor, and those who despise Me will be lightly esteemed. Behold, the days are coming when I will break your strength and the strength of your father's house so that there will not be an old man in your house.'" (2:27a, 29–31)

What had Eli and his sons done to deserve such a dire pronouncement? To begin with, Hophni and Phinehas were stealing the choice portions of the animal sacrifices and eating them for supper! They abused their position as priests through greed and, in other cases, even sexual immorality (see vv. 12–17, 22). As a result, the writer of 1 Samuel comments, "The sons of Eli were worthless men; they did not know the Lord" (v. 12).

And what was Eli doing while his sons ravaged God's house? Like the ho-hum, apathetic days in which he lived, Eli decided to sit back, fold his arms, and not make waves. With nothing more than a verbal reprimand (vv. 23–25), Eli closed his eyes to the whole affair until the Lord could be patient no longer.

Thus, God issues His final verdict to Samuel that quiet night—a horrifying pronouncement of judgment on Eli and his descendants forever.

> And the Lord said to Samuel, "Behold, I am about to do a thing in Israel at which both ears of everyone who hears it will tingle.[2] In that day I will carry out against Eli all that I have spoken concerning his house, from beginning to end. For I have told him that I am about to judge his house forever for the iniquity which he knew, because his sons brought a curse on themselves and he did not rebuke them. Therefore I have sworn to the house of Eli that the iniquity of Eli's house shall not be atoned for by sacrifice or offering forever." (3:11–14)

The words God gives Samuel are like the pounding of a mighty gavel. And the next morning, trying to go about his chores as usual, little Samuel is trembling at the thought of telling this vision to Eli. Eli, however, will not let him keep the secret, so Samuel relays

---

2. This expression conveys the idea that the news is so dreadful the people can't believe it. We might say, "It will take their breath away." See also 2 Kings 21:12 and Jeremiah 19:3.

the words of the Lord to him in detail. And Eli simply says, "It is the Lord; let Him do what seems good to Him" (v. 18b).

Eli's response is interesting. He resigns himself to accept God's will, but he still refuses to take action and discipline his sons.[3] They are left to do as they please, unrestrained.

It is also interesting that God did not tell Samuel to deliver the message to Eli. He just informed him of what would take place and left it at that. Perhaps it was a warning for Samuel not to follow in the footsteps of the two evil sons or the negligent father. Or perhaps the midnight Voice was a kind of confirmation of Samuel as a prophet (see v. 20). In any case, it was the way God chose to initiate communication with him, and Samuel was never the same.

Continuing Messages . . . Lessons Learned

The implications of God's words to Samuel jar our senses like an unexpected cymbal crash. God's judgment is never easy to hear, but if we listen to its ringing in our ears, we can learn valuable lessons for our lives.

Any Family Can Disintegrate

Eli's family was the spiritual guide for the nation, and the people revered them as honorable descendants of Aaron, the first high priest. Yet, as we have seen in our own day, even spiritual guides have weaknesses, and families that we think should be immune are often most susceptible to clay-feet disease. From this story, then, four signs of domestic disintegration are evident.

Number one: *Preoccupation with an occupation to the exclusion of family needs.* As the high priest, Eli nearly always faced a day full of spiritual busyness. He had to maintain his position in the community, and that meant working day and night. Keeping the ministry fed and well-groomed, he may have left little time for father-son camaraderie. As a result, Hophni and Phinehas drifted away from him and his God so that "they did not know the Lord" (2:12).

Number two: *Refusal to face the severity of children's actions.* Each time young Hophni's and Phinehas' defiant behavior went undisciplined, they made slow withdrawals from their character bank account. By the time they were adults, they were morally bankrupt

---

3. Eli's sin was that he did not discipline his defiant sons. As painful as it would have been to confront their disobedience, it could have spared the whole family God's severe discipline later (compare Deut. 21:18–21).

and had no resources whatsoever for making mature choices. Had Eli disciplined the boys while they were young, however, he would have invested in them character qualities that could have protected them against ruin. As Solomon advised: "Discipline your son in his early years while there is hope. If you don't you will ruin his life" (Prov. 19:18 LB).

Number three: *Failure to respond quickly and thoroughly to the warnings of others.* Eli was informed about his sons' behavior, but his impotent, sluggish response was nothing more than a watered-down warning (1 Sam. 2:22–25). Like Eli, we can be blind to our children's waywardness, but when the facts are known, we must respond immediately and appropriately.

Number four: *Rationalizing of wrong, thereby becoming part of the problem.* One telling verse describes Eli's attitude toward his sons' wickedness:

> "'Why do you kick at My sacrifice and at My offering which I have commanded in My dwelling, and honor your sons above Me, by making *yourselves* fat with the choicest of every offering of My people Israel?'"
> (v. 29, emphasis added)

Eli himself couldn't resist the scrumptious delights his sons stole from the animal sacrifices. In so doing, he was honoring his sons and dishonoring the Lord. As is often the case with families today, Eli's rationalizations spoke louder to his children than his religion.

This last sign of a disintegrating family brings us to our second lesson. The disobedience of Eli and his sons stands in contrast to Samuel's devotion to the Lord and illustrates the following principle.

Hearing the Truth Isn't Enough; Action Is Essential

Like no other family in Israel, Eli's family knew God's Word. Ignorance was not their problem; obedience was. Hophni and Phinehas ate God's Law like they ate the temple sacrifices: they grew fat on it, but it meant nothing to them.

In contrast, Samuel was teachable and obedient. And as a result, he was the one who directly heard God's voice. Venerable old Eli and his priest-sons should have been the ones invited to God's summit. But God chose to speak to a humble servant-boy clutching his covers in the darkness—the only one who could say, and mean it, "Speak, for Your servant is listening."

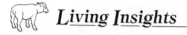

Billy Sunday was the king of the early twentieth-century revivalists. They built special tabernacles to hold the thousands who came to hear him; his name made front-page headlines wherever he went; his preaching even inspired the Prohibition Amendment. And after thirty-nine years of ministry, one hundred million Americans had heard him speak and over one million had come forward in response to his altar calls. Billy Sunday was a religious superstar.

But what about his family? In his day, it was an enormous task to organize such a large-scale ministry, requiring months of travel at a time. Billy and his wife worked feverishly, side by side. He often preached seven days a week, four times a day, while she took care of the mountain of administrative details. Their children? The oldest daughter was in college at the height of their ministry, but their three sons hit adolescence while mom and dad were on the road, busy saving America.

While Billy pounded the pulpit about moral responsibility, his irresponsible Hophni-and-Phinehas sons bounced in and out of trouble. They were constantly in debt, flagrantly promiscuous, and later had disastrous marriages. Two of their ex-wives even blackmailed the Sundays by threatening to go public with the embarrassing details. And, tragically, the oldest son committed suicide in 1933.

After his son's death, Billy pondered his busy life in a poignant moment with his wife, Nell.

> Billy stood gazing out the window of their Winona Lake home. Watching the autumn leaves fall, and looking wistfully toward the lake, he turned to her with tear-filled eyes and said, "Ma, where did I go wrong? I thought we heard God's call to evangelism. But look at our boys. Where did I go wrong?"[4]

None of us would like to reach the end of our lives—or our children's lives—tearfully wondering where we went wrong. But to avoid this, we have to do some tough thinking, starting now. Sincerely reflect on the following questions.

---

4. Lyle W. Dorsett, *Billy Sunday and the Redemption of Urban America* (Grand Rapids, Mich.: William B. Eerdmans Publishing Co., 1991), p. 132.

- Am I preoccupied with an occupation—work, church, community involvement—to the exclusion of my family's needs?

- Do I refuse to see the severity of my children's actions?

- Do I fail to respond quickly and thoroughly to the warnings of others?

- Am I rationalizing my children's wrongs, just becoming part of the problem?

If you see a crack developing in your family's foundation, it's not too late—repair is possible. Seek God's grace today, and ask Him to give you eyes to see the cracks and strength to begin again.

 ## Living Insights STUDY TWO

Many parents who have endured the agony of rebellious children have voiced Billy Sunday's question: "Where did we go wrong?" And like him, their first response may to be question God. "We did everything God told us to do. We took our kids to church and modeled right living. And now, God, look what we get in return. Pain and heartache from our children!"

We may think that if we sacrifice ourselves for God, then God will bless us with a happy family. And the more sacrifices we make, the more insurance we build up against disaster. But think about that logic for a minute. Do we really think that religiosity can buy God's protection?

God is not as interested in our religious activities as He is our family involvement. In light of our busy lifestyles, though, it is easy to ignore problems at home that may sap our time and energy. But dealing with those problems, while painful, is much more important than settling arguments in the music committee or negotiating sites for the church picnic.

- What has been soaking up your mental energy lately? Has your attention been properly balanced between outside concerns and family concerns? Think about the last few days and rate from one to ten, ten being high, the degree of mental energy that each area of life has been consuming in your mind.

     ___ Church/Ministry   ___ Marriage

     ___ Work   ___ Children

     ___ Friends   ___ Personal Walk

- If you feel out of balance, brainstorm some ways to refocus on family issues. Perhaps you could arrange a heart-to-heart talk with your spouse or call a family meeting. These are just some suggestions to help get you started. Feel free to be creative.

- Now, instead of focusing on past mistakes, ask yourself, "What can we do better?" What hot issues are you facing in your family? Write down the problem areas and also your ideas on how to improve them.

If you are feeling helpless concerning the difficult problems you are facing at home, we recommend the following resources: *The Strong Family*, by Charles R. Swindoll; *Boundaries with Kids*, by Henry Cloud and John Townsend; *The Five Love Languages of Children*, by Gary Chapman and Ross Campbell; and for the unique problems single parents face, *Successful Single Parenting*, by Gary Richmond.

Chapter 6

THE TEENAGER WHO WHIPPED A GIANT
1 Samuel 17:1–54

Judgment at Nuremberg is a cinematic masterpiece, intelligent and eloquent. Set in 1948, the film revolves around the trial of four German judges who have been indicted for their participation in Nazi atrocities. The crux of the film is the issue of moral responsibility, but it also paints a subtle yet penetrating contrast between the power of Hitler's followers and the helplessness of his victims.

After listening to the disquieting opening remarks of the prosecution and defense, the presiding judge, played by Spencer Tracy, goes for a walk around historic Nuremberg. He is taken by the city's charm—until he reaches the arena where so many Nazi rallies had been held. With his eyes on the vast stands and the platform where Hitler had screamed out his hateful messages, the judge hears the ghostly voices of that fateful place. The shouts and cheers of the tremendous throng rise and swell, finally giving way to the voice of Hitler himself. Tracy's character is struck by the ferocity of the pride, the immensity of the power.

Later, back in the courtroom, the prosecution shows films of concentration camps. Silently, image after image of starved men and babies, emaciated bodies of the nameless dead heaped in piles, and charred remains in the crematoriums testify to the horror of the crimes and the helplessness of Hitler's victims.

The deafening pride of the powerful on one hand, the silent victimization of the helpless on the other.

Yet the story is not new to this century, not unique to Germany or to World War II. Instead, it's one repeated through the ages. The story we will study today retells this old tale, with the powerful and merciless Philistines shouting their arrogant threats at the quaking, silent Israelites . . . ironically, God's people.

The Scene of the Battle

The age-old enemies of God's people, the brutish Philistines, have once again entered Israel, this time planting themselves on a hilltop overlooking the Elah valley (1 Sam. 17:1–2). This large and fertile farmland, with a ravine running through the middle, is one of the strategic gateways to the hill country of Israel. As the two armies eye each other across the valley (v. 3), the Philistine ranks suddenly part, and a certain mountain of a man steps forward.

The Two Major Opponents

To avoid an all-out battle, the Philistines choose a one-on-one confrontation between two champions instead. So, thinking, "How could we lose?" they chuckle to themselves as they roll out their one-man armored division to challenge the trembling Israelites.

A Philistine Giant Named Goliath

The earth seems to shake as Goliath rumbles out within shouting distance and stands to his full nine feet, nine inches. He is an armor-plated, fully loaded fighting machine.[1] Squaring his huge shoulders, he bellows up to the Israelites who are peeking over the ridge:

> "Choose a man for yourselves and let him come down to me. If he is able to fight with me and kill me, then we will become your servants; but if I prevail against him and kill him, then you shall become our servants and serve us." (vv. 8b–9)

Every morning and evening for forty days, Goliath issues his challenge (v. 16). Who will be Israel's champion? Shouldn't King Saul fight this pagan blasphemer (see 8:20)? After all, he is the tallest, strongest man in Israel (9:2). Yet he cowers along with the rest of the soldiers in the enormous shadow of the Philistine (17:11).[2]

A Jewish Shepherd Named David

From the bellowing of Goliath to the bleating of sheep, the scriptural scene shifts to a tranquil hill outside Bethlehem. David, the youngest of eight sons, shepherds the family flocks while his three oldest brothers are at the battle site. Concerned about his

---

1. Goliath's armor consisted of bronze leg protectors and a coat of mail made of bronze ringlets woven on thick fabric. The weight of his armor was about two hundred pounds, and the iron head of his oversized javelin weighed twenty-five pounds. Goliath was also accompanied by an armor bearer who would carry a shield to defend against arrows.

2. Not only did Saul show his cowardice by not fighting Goliath, he also showed his desperation by offering a reward to anyone who would fight him. The prize was riches, marriage to his daughter, and tax exemption for life (1 Sam. 17:25).

boys' welfare, David's father sends him down to the Elah valley to deliver food and check on them (vv. 12–19).

Once there, David catches his first glimpse of Goliath, who is busy making his daily taunt. David also sees his fellow Israelites trembling in fear (vv. 20–24). His mind races with questions: Why is everyone afraid of this *giant?* Does God not hear his defiance too? Will He not come to our rescue? That miscreant may be big, but to God he is a mere fly, and I will be His flyswatter!

David looked at the threatening situation through the Lord's eyes and was therefore able to see past outward appearances. He saw Goliath's wicked heart, and that was the important issue—not his size. David's attitude here is a living illustration of God's earlier words to Samuel: "God sees not as man sees, for man looks at the outward appearance, but the Lord looks at the heart" (16:7b).

Knowing the Lord's character and power, David also realizes that God's patience is running out with the loudmouth giant. So he makes his move and starts questioning the soldiers around him:

> "What will be done for the man who kills this Phi-
> listine and takes away the reproach from Israel? For
> who is this uncircumcised Philistine, that he should
> taunt the armies of the living God?" (17:26)

Brave, inspiring, commendable words, aren't they? But not to David's oldest brother, who accuses him of youthful arrogance.

> Now Eliab his oldest brother heard when he spoke
> to the men; and Eliab's anger burned against David
> and he said, "Why have you come down? And with
> whom have you left those few sheep in the wilder-
> ness? I know your insolence and the wickedness of
> your heart; for you have come down in order to see
> the battle." (v. 28)

The Living Bible paraphrases Eliab's words this way: "I know what a cocky brat you are!" Sounds like an older-brother comment, doesn't it? How true it is that as soon as you start stepping out in the strength of the Lord, somebody will want to put you down—often your own family.

Unfortunately, though, sometimes we are that sarcastic some-body. But if we're not able to face the giant ourselves, we need to stop criticizing others who, like David, trust God and prepare to do battle.

Word eventually grapevines to Saul that someone is talking big about facing the giant. So David is led to the king, and the following interchange takes place:

> And David said to Saul, "Let no man's heart fail on account of him; your servant will go and fight with this Philistine." Then Saul said to David, "You are not able to go against this Philistine to fight with him; for you are but a youth while he has been a warrior from his youth." (vv. 32–33)

Saul saw only a giant, but David saw only the Lord. And unlike Saul, David never forgot the past victories the Lord had given him.

> But David said to Saul, "Your servant was tending his father's sheep. When a lion or a bear came and took a lamb from the flock, I went out after him and attacked him, and rescued it from his mouth; and when he rose up against me, I seized him by his beard and struck him and killed him . . . .The Lord who delivered me from the paw of the lion and from the paw of the bear, He will deliver me from the hand of this Philistine." (vv. 34–35, 37a)

Saul says, "Go, and may the Lord be with you" (v. 37b), but his next actions betray a lack of faith:

> Then Saul clothed David with his garments and put a bronze helmet on his head, and he clothed him with armor. (v. 38)

Politely, David tries it on; but the armor made for the tallest man in Israel just doesn't fit the boy shepherd. And here we learn an important lesson: We can't meet our Goliaths in someone else's strength because what works for them may not work for us. We have to be who we are, which is just what David does. Armed with his sling, some rocks, and a stick, he heads down into the valley . . . alone (vv. 39–40).

The Actual Contest

Both hilltops now come alive with commotion. Like spectators at a world-class boxing match, the crowd electrifies and all eyes rivet on the two combatants who enter the ring.

Warming Up

At first the taunting was fun, but Goliath is now impatient, wanting to get on with the killing and start enjoying the spoils of victory. But what's this? A boy with sticks and stones? Killing this boy would be nothing; the sight of him angers Goliath and insults his pride. So he mocks David and curses him by his gods (vv. 41–44).

Speaking Up

But David is not intimidated.

> Then David said to the Philistine, "You come to me with a sword, a spear, and a javelin, but I come to you in the name of the Lord of hosts, the God of the armies of Israel, whom you have taunted. This day the Lord will deliver you up into my hands, and I will strike you down and remove your head from you. . . . that all the earth may know that there is a God in Israel, and that all this assembly may know that the Lord does not deliver by sword or by spear; for the battle is the Lord's and He will give you into our hands." (vv. 45–47)

David's philosophy speaks loud and clear. It isn't the intimidation that comes from without that wins the battle—the visible, tangible weapons. *It is the faith that comes from within.* That is what is significant when we meet the Goliaths in our life. "The battle is the Lord's"—and our part is to trust His power.

Mopping Up

Whiz.

This is the last sound Goliath hears before David's fastball hits him right between the running lights. The giant falls dead, and the frightened Philistines kick up dust running for home.

Then, taking Goliath's sword, David severs the giant's head and carries it "to Jerusalem, but he put [Goliath's] weapons in his tent" (v. 54). They are now mute reminders of another victory; they, like the jawbone of a certain lion and the skin of a certain bear, are David's testimonies to God's faithfulness, might, and power.

Things to Remember When Fighting Today's Giants

The story of David and Goliath is reassuring because we all face giants in our lives. They may not be nine feet, nine inches tall; they may not even be people. They may involve fears, difficult circumstances like unemployment, or worries about the future. But while we are standing on the hilltop overlooking our own Elah valley, it will be helpful to remember these important truths.

Facing giants is an intimidating experience. Your giant may be a trip to the hospital, the breakup of your family, or even a horrible past with memories you just can't shake. All these things are as intimidating as a dark alley in the bad part of town. And it's OK to acknowledge your own fear.

Doing battle is a lonely experience. Although others may be near to support you, the battle is ultimately between you and the giant. But in the midst of the loneliness, you will experience the strength of God. Although you feel lonely, you are not alone.

Trusting God is a reassuring experience. In the midst of your darkest hour, God is there. What a comfort to experience the warmth of His presence, which stops the shivering and sends away the chill.

Winning victories is a memorable experience. David could face a giant because he had already faced a lion and a bear. Faith cultivated in the smaller challenges ripens into confidence to handle life's giants.

One Concluding Reminder

Never underestimate the power of God, and stop overestimating the confidence of the enemy. Many of the giants that we face are powerless, for they are nothing more than empty shells, having no substance at all. And what gives the story of David so much impact is that deep within his life there is substance . . . there is truth. And there's nothing like a pocketful of truth when facing giants.

 Living Insights

It's Monday morning and the house bustles like Grand Central Station. Dad has already caught the express into town, the kids are downing their breakfast, and mom is taking care of a few spills. Her mind is a switchboard of thoughts: a quick glance at the clock, a few orders prefaced by "please," and trains 2 through 5 are poised for departure.

Then the doorbell rings.

"Hop in the car, I'll be right there. And don't forget your

lunches," she calls. *Who could it be at this time of morning?* Turning the knob, a blast of wind pushes the door open and swirls a dust cloud around her feet. She looks up and there he stands, all nine feet, nine inches of him—her unexpected giant.

"What . . . ?" She stands blinking for a moment; then, addressing the giant in a hushed voice, "Look, I . . . I really don't have time . . ."

The giant throws her a curious grin and then squeezes through the door. Taking two seconds to size up the house, he lumbers to the family room and, like a long-lost uncle, stuffs himself into dad's chair.

After a moment, he turns his head and sees her standing like a statue in the hallway. "Got any pretzels?" he says and lets out a belly laugh that shakes the whole house.

Unexpected and definitely unwanted, our giant always barges in at the worst possible moment and always stays longer than we wish—sometimes years. What is your giant? Here are few possibilities:

Unemployment	Illness	Lust
Depression	Death	Self-doubt
Alcoholism	Loneliness	Regret

Have any of these disrupting giants lumbered into your house? Goliath had five brothers—maybe a whole family of giants has moved in to stay! Can you name them?

_____   _____

_____   _____

How have you dealt with them? Have you faced them in faith, like David? Run from them, like the Israelites? Tried to get somebody else to fight them, like Saul? What strategy have you followed most often?

_____

_____

_____

_____

Is there a certain aspect of facing your giants that may be hindering your efforts—perhaps intimidation or loneliness? Write down what you struggle with most in the battle.

_____

_____

_____

Whatever your giants are, don't despair. If Goliath could be toppled, so can your giant. Trust God; after all, it is really His battle. Take a moment and commit your giants to the Lord, recognizing God's power to defeat them. Then go on to Study Two, where you can start your giant-killing plan of attack.

 ## _Living Insights_

Giants are intimidating—that's their job. And it's OK to feel frightened. However, when fear immobilizes us so that we stand trembling at every threatening word, we have forgotten about the power of God. And we have forgotten about the sling in our hand and the stones in our pocket.

God offers us His strength to do battle with our giants, but He also has given us slings and stones—resources to use in the fight. What giant-killing weapons has God issued you? Write down one of the giants you listed in Study One. Then do a brief inspection of your God-given armory and write down the resources available to you for the fight.

My giant: _____

My weapons: _____

_____

_____

Young David's story teaches us that faith-inspired action is essential when killing giants. Our weapons are useless if they are left on the shelf, and victory is always a dream if we sit quietly on the hilltop. Today is the day for action. What do you think God is telling you to do with the resources He has given you? How are you going to use them? When do you think it can be accomplished? Take some time to think through your battle plan; then write it down.

My battle plan: _____

_____

_____

_____

_____

Now, before you close this chapter, pray for God's strength in the fight. You know what the enemy is, you know what your resources are, and you know what you need to do. Now you need power. The following prayer of Patrick of Ireland expresses his dependence on the power of God. Claim it for yourself, and remember, the battle belongs to the Lord.[3]

> I bind unto myself today
> The power of God to hold and lead,
> His eye to watch, his might to stay,
> His ear to hearken to my need.
> The wisdom of my God to teach,
> His hand to guide, his shield to ward;
> The word of God to give me speech,
> His heavenly host to be my guard.[4]

---

3. For further help in giant killing, we highly recommend the following: *Trusting God*, by Jerry Bridges; and *Killing Giants, Pulling Thorns*, by Charles R. Swindoll.

4. Patrick of Ireland, as quoted in *The One Year Book of Personal Prayer* (Wheaton, Ill.: Tyndale House Publishers, 1991), p. 4.

Chapter 7

THE WOMAN WHO SAVED HER HUSBAND'S NECK

1 Samuel 25:1–42

A man discovers a priceless masterpiece hidden behind a painting he paid ten dollars for at an estate sale. A woman looks inside her great-grandfather's violin and reads the name of its maker, Antonio Stradivari. A boy opens a box of old, dusty toys his father is about to throw out, and he sees tucked in the corner a baseball card. With wide eyes, he reads: Mickey Mantle, rookie.

People dream about discovering treasures such as these. But what if the ones who found these prizes didn't care about them? What if the man rolled up the priceless painting and tossed it in the garage? Or the woman—what if she nailed the Stradivarius to the wall as a decoration? Or what if the boy stuck the Mickey Mantle card to a board and used it as a target for darts?

Just thinking about it makes us cringe. But it did happen, in a way, in our story today. The treasure isn't an object, however; it is a woman named Abigail. She is a sparkling gem of integrity and virtue, but she is married to a brutish husband named Nabal, who devalues her even though she bravely saves his life. Fortunately, her story does have a happy ending because of a certain surprising turn of events. Curious? Read on and we'll introduce you to the main characters of our drama.

Meeting the Main Characters of the Story

As the curtain rises for the first act of our story, we meet the three main characters: the hero, the villain, and the heroine. David is the handsome hero, and he first occupies center stage.

David

> Then Samuel died; and all Israel gathered together and mourned for him, and buried him at his house in Ramah. And David arose and went down to the wilderness of Paran. (1 Sam. 25:1)

Getting a feel for our historical setting is essential to understanding the story. To begin with, the prophet Samuel had anointed

David as king-elect of Israel years before, but David subsequently had to run for his life from jealous King Saul. In fact, as we begin our story, he has just encountered Saul at Engedi, where he mercifully spared the old king's life (chap. 24). As a result, Saul calls off the manhunt for a while, and now David and his six hundred trained fighting men roam the wilderness of Paran, attempting to scratch out a living.

Rather than becoming desperados, David and his men employ themselves as police, protecting the local ranchers and their herds of sheep from thieves and wild animals. No formal contracts are signed because it is customary for the ranchers to remunerate the volunteer force for their services. Only a tightfisted miser would refuse to pay.

Like Nabal, the villain in our drama.

Nabal

> Now there was a man in Maon whose business was in Carmel; and the man was very rich, and he had three thousand sheep and a thousand goats. (25:2a)

This rich man's name is Nabal, which means "fool." The name is fitting not so much because he is an ignorant dolt but because he is vulgar, ill-natured, and belligerent. His selfish and stingy heart spews prejudice and stubborn pride. And in his clutches is our heroine, his wife, Abigail.

Abigail

> Now the man's name was Nabal, and his wife's name was Abigail. And the woman was intelligent and beautiful in appearance, but the man was harsh and evil in his dealings, and he was a Calebite. (v. 3)

Intelligent and attractive, Abigail far outshines her harsh, foolish husband. How did two so obviously mismatched people wind up married? Probably, their marriage was arranged by their parents when they were children. Sometimes this works; other times, such as with Nabal and Abigail, it is disastrous. But this remarkable woman retains her dignity despite her husband's churlishness, as we shall see as our plot unfolds.

Following the Plot of the Story

David, absorbed in day-to-day survival, is unaware of Abigail. But a set of unusual circumstances will soon bring her to his attention.

A Request for Remuneration

For months, David and his men have been voluntarily watching over Nabal's sheep and herdsmen. When they hear that Nabal has begun shearing the sheep in order to market the wool, they decide it is time to collect their gratuity. So David sends ten emissaries to politely remind Nabal of his obligations (vv. 4–5a). He isn't pushy or grasping in his message; in fact, he is extremely gracious.

> "Go up to Carmel, visit Nabal and greet him in my name; and thus you shall say, 'Have a long life, peace be to you, and peace be to your house, and peace be to all that you have. Now I have heard that you have shearers; now your shepherds have been with us and we have not insulted them, nor have they missed anything all the days they were in Carmel. Ask your young men and they will tell you. Therefore let my young men find favor in your eyes, for we have come on a festive day. Please give whatever you find at hand to your servants and to your son David.'"
>
> When David's young men came, they spoke to Nabal according to all these words in David's name; then they waited. (vv. 5b–9)

But Nabal, with a smirk, replies:

> "Who is David? And who is the son of Jesse? There are many servants today who are each breaking away from his master. Shall I then take my bread and my water and my meat that I have slaughtered for my shearers, and give it to men whose origin I do not know?" (vv. 10b–11)

Profane Nabal thinks nothing of snubbing the Lord's anointed. And the ten men return to David empty-handed, wondering how David will react (v. 12).

A Plan for Retaliation

Feeling the sting of Nabal's slap in his face, David, who had reined in his vengeance with Saul at Engedi, now rashly arms for a swift and bloody reprisal (v. 13).

Meanwhile, back at the ranch, Abigail finds out from an unnamed servant about Nabal's foolish rebuff of David's men.

> "Behold, David sent messengers from the wilderness to greet our master, and he scorned them. Yet the men were very good to us. . . . They were a wall to us both by night and by day, all the time we were with them tending the sheep. Now therefore, know and consider what you should do, for evil is plotted against our master and against all his household; and he is such a worthless man that no one can speak to him." (vv. 14b–15a, 16–17)

Abigail does not have to "consider" long, for she knows what she has to do. Now she may have been tempted to think, "My, but God works in mysterious ways! Let's pray that my dear husband's passing will be swift and painless." But instead, she wisely considers the painful consequences of David's rash act, not only for her "worthless" husband, but also for David, whose reputation as the soon-to-be king needs protecting. So, without Nabal's knowing it, she puts her plan into action.

An Act of Intercession

First, she quickly whips up a feast to give David and his men and courageously rides off to intercept them in the hills (vv. 18–20). Spying the band rumbling across the desert, she tactfully plays the peacemaker.

> When Abigail saw David, she hurried and dismounted from her donkey, and fell on her face before David and bowed herself to the ground. She fell at his feet and said, "On me alone, my lord, be the blame. And please let your maidservant speak to you, and listen to the words of your maidservant. Please do not let my lord pay attention to this worthless man, Nabal, for as his name is, so is he. Nabal is his name and folly is with him; but I your maidservant did not see the young men of my lord whom you sent.
> Now therefore, my lord, as the Lord lives, and as your soul lives, since the Lord has restrained you

from shedding blood, and from avenging yourself by your own hand, now then let your enemies and those who seek evil against my lord, be as Nabal. Now let this gift which your maidservant has brought to my lord be given to the young men who accompany my lord. Please forgive the transgression of your maidservant; for the Lord will certainly make for my lord an enduring house, because my lord is fighting the battles of the Lord, and evil will not be found in you all your days." (vv. 23–28)

With remarkable diplomacy and selflessness, she pours oil on troubled waters, taking the blame for Nabal's offense and asking for David's forgiveness. And with each word, David's vengeful heart softens.

Finally, in her closing appeal, Abigail displays her devotion to the Lord when she expresses her desire to see God's will accomplished in David's life.

"And when the Lord does for my lord according to all the good that He has spoken concerning you, and appoints you ruler over Israel, this will not cause grief or a troubled heart to my lord, both by having shed blood without cause and by my lord having avenged himself. When the Lord shall deal well with my lord, then remember your maidservant." (vv. 30–31)

With those words, Abigail waits quietly for David's response. The ruddy warrior shifts uneasily in his saddle, thinking about his hotheaded vow to kill Nabal (vv. 21–22)—a vow he now wishes he had never made. But, characteristic of his godly humility, David unhesitatingly submits to what he knows is the truth.

Then David said to Abigail, "Blessed be the Lord God of Israel, who sent you this day to meet me, and blessed be your discernment, and blessed be you, who have kept me this day from bloodshed and from avenging myself by my own hand. Nevertheless, as the Lord God of Israel lives, who has restrained me from harming you, unless you had come quickly to meet me, surely there would not have been left to Nabal until the morning light as much as one male." So David received from her hand what she had brought him and said to her, "Go up to your house in peace. See, I have listened to you and granted your request." (vv. 32–35)

Whew! Her work is done and she turns for home. Home . . . and Nabal.

A Surprising Conclusion

Tired and emotionally spent, Abigail walks in the front door of her home and into the arms of a grateful husband.

Unfortunately, that's not how the story goes. Rather, she stumbles onto an appalling scene:

> Then Abigail came to Nabal, and behold, he was holding a feast in his house, like the feast of a king. And Nabal's heart was merry within him, for he was very drunk; so she did not tell him anything at all until the morning light. (v. 36)

The next morning, she approaches her hungover husband and paints a picture of the events of the past day. Then, suddenly and ironically, Nabal's heart, which for so long had been hard toward her and the Lord, "died within him so that he became as a stone" (v. 37b). Apparently, he went into a coma, and ten days later, he was dead (v. 38). So ends the life of this miserly man.

But there's more. Watch David's response to Nabal's death.

> When David heard that Nabal was dead, he said, "Blessed be the Lord, who has pleaded the cause of my reproach from the hand of Nabal and has kept back His servant from evil. The Lord has also returned the evildoing of Nabal on his own head." Then David sent a proposal to Abigail, to take her as his wife. (v. 39)

And Abigail wastes no time in accepting David's proposal of marriage (v. 42). A romantic end to one woman's story of courage and grace.

Learning Some Lessons from the Story

Who would have thought such romance existed in the pages of the Old Testament? Abigail's story warms us, but it also teaches us some valuable lessons.

61

From David, we learn that *rash reactions never pay off.* "Never take your own revenge, beloved, but leave room for the wrath of God" (Rom. 12:19a). We are wise to cool our thoughts of retaliation and trust the Lord to handle the Nabals of our lives.

From Nabal, we learn that *insensitive husbands always leave unknown heartaches in their wake.* Nabal insensibly scorned David, whom he owed a great debt; he was oblivious to the danger his attitude caused for his family; and he was insensitive to Abigail's need for affirmation. If you are a Nabal, wake up! Break that habit of turning a deaf ear. For if you don't, you'll leave a legacy of heartaches behind you.

From Abigail, we learn that *wise wives seldom miss the best use of timing and tact.* When she sensed danger, Abigail acted swiftly; when she faced the murder in David's eyes, her words were kind and calm. And when she returned home, she remained silent for the best opportunity to confront Nabal. Then she explained everything openly.

The beauty of this story is the reminder that sometimes fairy tales do come true and that the Lord does want to give us the desires of our hearts when we delight ourselves in Him (Ps. 37:4). It's a hope to cling to and a promise to believe.

 Living Insights

Wanting to Follow, Forced to Lead—it's the title of a book that describes the dilemma faced by women who are chained to Nabal-type men in marriage. In the book, the author describes the frustration of such a situation as she writes about a woman named Jenny.

> She wanted to follow what she understood to be the biblical pattern of a submissive wife, but how did one do that with a passive, nonassertive husband . . . ? She wanted to be a full-time mother, but he was hinting more strongly every day that she should return to work. She wanted a strong Christian father for her children, but Ted had never once sat down with them and opened a Bible. He could find time to go on a fishing trip with a six-pack of beer and his friends, but she and the children could

never be worked into his schedule.[1]

If you identify with Jenny's predicament of living with an insensitive mate, then take a closer look at Abigail. Ask this question: How did she survive her one-sided relationship?

First, reread 1 Samuel 25 and note her actions and attitudes. Did she deny what her husband was really like? Did she exaggerate his defects to humiliate him? Did she nag or manipulate him? Write down what you observe.

_____

_____

_____

_____

Now examine your observations of Abigail and write down any principles that speak to your situation.

_____

_____

_____

_____

How can you apply these principles to your life?

_____

_____

_____

Of course, the Lord snapped Abigail's chain to Nabal in an unusual way. Had God not intervened, though, her strategy of dealing with Nabal would have taken her through many difficult years. May the Lord give you the strength to endure and may your trust in Him grow because He knows, even better than you, the desires of your heart.

1. Elizabeth Baker, *Wanting to Follow, Forced to Lead* (Wheaton, Ill.: Tyndale House Publishers, 1991), p. vii.

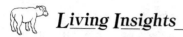

Shifting our attention from Abigail to David, let's play "worst-case scenario." What if David *had* taken revenge?

- What would David have been guilty of (1 Sam. 25:26, 31)?

  _____

- What prerogative would he have taken from God (vv. 26, 31)?

  _____

- What would he have sacrificed (vv. 28, 30)?

  _____

- What would he have gained (v. 31)?

  _____

All because of an impassioned moment of hotheaded revenge.

Has someone offended you lately, sparking a flame of revenge in your heart? If so, what was the situation?

_____

_____

Suffering an offense from a family member, friend, boss, or co-worker naturally pricks our retaliation instincts. But before you know it, a small flame of revenge can grow into an all-consuming blaze, burning yourself and others. What worst-case scenario may result if you try to "even the score"?

_____

_____

_____

David wisely followed Abigail's advice to not "pay attention to this worthless man, Nabal" (v. 25). Should this be your course of action concerning your offending Nabal? In so doing, you'll be trusting the Lord to resolve the problem—a much better scenario.

Chapter 8

THE UNKNOWN WHO BECAME WELL-KNOWN

1 Chronicles 4:9–10

Galloping into battle in his bright green cavalry jacket and his polished riding boots, "Light Horse Harry" was the soul of the American Revolution. With his Virginian air of command and horseman's gallantry, his exploits made him a lieutenant colonel and gained him the respect of Washington, Hamilton, and Madison. His name was legendary—everyone knew the glory stories about the fighting days of Light Horse Harry.

When the war ended, he assumed the quiet life of a country gentleman, marrying a plantation heiress and serving as a governor as well as in Congress. But he burned inside. A dreamer and a gambler, he took big investment risks; unfortunately, he accumulated more debt than fortune. When his wife of five years died, he married another daughter of wealth, Ann Carter, whose star-filled eyes were quickly opened to her husband's true nature.

Ever chasing elusive schemes and speculations, he constantly strayed from Ann and the children. To pay his debts, he sold her land, horses, slaves—everything. Then, to make matters more difficult, Ann discovered she was pregnant again. She already had five children to care for by herself; how could she handle a sixth? Without money to even keep the house warm, she lay desperately ill, and once wrote to her sister-in-law that she dearly wished not to have this baby. But on January 19, Ann's baby was born, a boy whom she named after her two brothers Robert and Edward . . . a boy who grew up to be the legendary Robert E. Lee.[1]

An unwanted baby and the son of a man he never knew, young Robert was born into a world of pain. But that did not destroy his spirit. For he learned to rise above his past, like the main character of another story we will examine today. This was a man who was

---

This lesson is based on J. Oswald Sanders' chapter "God-Sanctioned Ambition," from *A Spiritual Clinic* (Chicago, Ill.: Moody Press, 1958), pp. 97–104.

1. Gene Smith, *Lee and Grant: A Dual Biography* (New York, N.Y.: McGraw-Hill Book Co., 1984), pp. 1–7.

also born with pain—whose name even means "pain"—a man called Jabez.

A Background of Darkness and Death

Tucked away in the pages of your Bible is Jabez's story, recorded in two verses of the book of 1 Chronicles.

The Historical Times

The chronicler who tells us about Jabez paints a broad landscape of the joys and sorrows of God's people as he traces Jewish history, beginning with Adam. Throughout his record, he emphasizes God's faithfulness in bringing the people through the dark times when enemies, like the Babylonians, constantly threatened the small nation.

The Scriptural Context

And as the chronicler writes about the Davids and the Hezekiahs of Judah's history, he does not the forget the lesser-knowns. For in the middle of a nine-chapter-long genealogy that seems to go on like rows of tombstones in a cemetery, he pauses by the grave of one man who never was a king, never was a prophet, but whose epitaph bears recognition. As J. Oswald Sanders wrote,

> When God troubles to preserve the epitaph of one man out of millions and gives it in such concise and meaningful language, we can be certain that it will repay detailed study.[2]

So we will pause to admire this man who, although dead, has etched a momentary, meteoric streak across the dark sky of Judah's history.

A Story of Faith and Hope

That brief yet brilliant streak of light made by Jabez's life is recorded in 1 Chronicles 4:9–10.

> Jabez was more honorable than his brothers, and his mother named him Jabez saying, "Because I bore him with pain." Now Jabez called on the God of

2. Sanders, *A Spiritual Clinic*, p. 101.

Israel, saying, "Oh that You would bless me indeed and enlarge my border, and that Your hand might be with me, and that You would keep me from harm that it may not pain me!" And God granted him what he requested.

In just two verses, the chronicler tells us volumes about Jabez's story, a story of faith and hope that first highlights his unusual name.

His Name

Throughout his life, Jabez's name, meaning "pain,"[3] was a burden he carried. It immediately separated him from others whose names meant "valiant one" or "dear one." Instead, Jabez knew that he was the "one who causes pain." Why would his mother give him that negative label?

His Birth

The chronicler tells us that his mother named him Jabez because she "bore him with pain." Apparently, the circumstances of his birth were distressful to her, and his arrival only illustrated that sorrow.

Could the painful circumstances have been similar to those surrounding Robert E. Lee's birth? Maybe Jabez's arrival burdened the family because they were in poverty. Perhaps, like Ann Carter Lee, Jabez's mother did not want another baby. Was her husband also a scoundrel? Maybe Jabez's mother was ill or his father died just before his birth.

Whatever the situation, every time he heard his name, he was reminded that his birth caused pain to his mother and to his family. As a result, "in a day when names were felt to have an effect upon the character and experience of their bearers,"[4] he grew up with a devastating, negative self-image.

Yet, as Scripture records, he became an honorable man,[5] more honorable than his brothers (v. 9a). What was it that freed him

---

3. The name Jabez, *Yabets* in Hebrew, is related to the word for "pain," "sorrow," or "grief"— *otseb*. So the name implies "He causes sorrow." See *The Wycliffe Bible Commentary*, ed. Charles F. Pfeiffer and Everett F. Harrison (Chicago, Ill.: Moody Press, 1962), p. 372.

4. J. G. McConville, *1 and 2 Chronicles*, The Daily Study Bible Series, ed. John C. L. Gibson (Philadelphia, Pa.: Westminster Press, 1984), p. 10.

5. The word is the passive form of the Hebrew verb *kabed*. It means literally, "to be made heavy." The implication is that Jabez was influential and his words and wishes carried weight in the community in which he lived.

from the choke hold his name and its implications had on his life? How could he, who began life two steps behind, become an honored and respected leader of men?

His Prayer

The turning point in Jabez's life came when he "called on the God of Israel" (v. 10a). In the Lord he discovered his Creator, the One who formed him in his mother's womb—not with sorrow but with delight. So, in faith, he called on Him in prayer. And the Lord listened.

In his prayer, Jabez made four requests. And we can voice these same requests when we experience a holy desire to rise above our circumstances. Let's look at them together.

His first plea was for divine ennoblement. Jabez pleaded with the Lord, "Oh that You would bless me indeed." By using the word "indeed," he showed his earnest desire for God's highest blessing, one that would elevate him above his tragic beginnings and bestow on him qualities of excellence.

Next, he requested divine enlargement, praying, "Enlarge my border." He wanted the Lord to break the limitations of his past and expand his power and influence. Such ambition, which challenges overwhelming odds, is not self-aggrandizement; rather, it represents a holy fire to glorify God on a larger scale. J. Oswald Sanders wrote:

> "Attempt great things for God. Expect great things from God" [William Carey]. God is looking for men who, like Jabez, are discontented with a limited opportunity when they could bring greater glory to God in a wider sphere. Our ambition should be for a wider influence for God, a deeper love toward God, a stronger faith in God and a growing knowledge of God.[6]

Allowing anxieties and restrictions from our past to cement us to a small sphere of influence can repress God's larger design for us. Like Jabez, we must break free from those limitations and pray for God to enlarge our borders as well.

Third, he asked for divine empowerment. Jabez knew that if God expanded his influence, then he must also pray, "Oh . . . that Your

---

6. Sanders, *A Spiritual Clinic*, p. 103.

hand might be with me." Traveling in our own strength is a miserable journey. We may walk in dependence on the Lord at first, but later we may wander, becoming overconfident and self-reliant. Jabez knew that such wandering away from the Lord would be dangerous, so he humbly prayed for God's guiding presence.

Last, Jabez wanted divine enablement, asking, "That You would keep me from harm." He sought God's power not only to guide him but also to protect him. After this final request, Jabez expressed his underlying motivation when he said, "That it may not pain me!" The purpose behind his ambition was a deep yearning to be free from the shackles of his past. He wanted to be free from his name— no longer a man of pain, but a man worthy of the Lord's blessings.

The Result

Jabez's heartfelt prayer moved the Lord, for as the chronicler simply notes, "God granted him what he requested." And through that answered prayer, the Lord elevated Jabez above his brothers as an honored and respected man in Israel.

Three Lessons and a Question

If the patterns of pessimism in Jabez's past match yours, then consider the following lessons his life teaches and the question it asks. God may be calling you to a greater sphere of influence than you ever imagined possible.

One: A small, struggling start doesn't necessitate a limited life. If we're not careful, the adversary may convince us that we should expect our future to be no different from our past. "You have to live with your restrictions" is the devil's message. But God's message contradicts that: "You can live beyond your restrictions through Me."

Two: No measure of success is safe without the presence of God's hand on a life. Living beyond our past and becoming a success is only half the battle. Jabez wisely requested that the Lord protect him once he achieved his place of honor. How many strong Christians have fallen once they achieved power because they flaunted it and were destroyed by it? Instead, we need to continually recognize and rely upon God's protective hand to shield us from enemy attacks that come from without and within.

Three: When it is God who prospers and blesses a life, there is no place for guilt. Occupying a place of honor not only requires God's protection from pride, but it also requires God's protection from false guilt. Others with selfish motives may envy God's place of honor for us, and they may heap mounds of false guilt upon us. But if God has ushered us from pain to blessing, from shame to honor, then should people convince us that it is wrong? Rather, as long as God is glorified in our success, we need not feel ashamed.

Like all good stories, this story of Jabez also leaves us with a question to ask ourselves: *"What large thing am I asking of God these days?"* Maybe you have expected too little of yourself because you cannot escape your feelings of inadequacy. Maybe you have never even imagined God could use you more. Maybe you need to bow before the Lord like Jabez and plead to be set free from the burden of your past, to be used by Him in new and larger ways. Who knows what blessings are stored in heaven, locked away when ignored but abundantly available when requested? Maybe some are waiting for you.

But you will never know unless you ask.

 ## Living Insights

At the brink of the American Civil War, before Robert E. Lee's home state, Virginia, seceded from the Union, Lee said, "I can anticipate no greater calamity for the country than a dissolution of the Union. I am willing to sacrifice everything but honour for its preservation." But if Lee believed in the Union, why did he become a general in the Confederate army?

He did not fight for slavery, for he had said long before, "Slavery as an institution is a moral and political evil." Neither did he fight for love of war: "What a cruel thing is war," he wrote to his wife, "to separate and destroy families and friends, and mar the purest joys and happiness God has granted us in this world."[7]

He fought for honor—the honor of his home state, his friends, and his family whom he could not turn against. As a result, the son of "Light Horse Harry" Lee—who had little sense of morality or responsibility—became an honorable man.

Like Lee, Jabez was born with a reproach on his name. But he rose above it to become honorable and respected. What about your past? What reproaches or pains do you bear?

---

7. Smith, *Lee and Grant*, pp. 80, 88, 157.

_____

_____

_____

How has the past limited your pursuit of a higher calling?

_____

_____

_____

_____

Although you may not be a general in charge of the fates of thousands, the Lord may want you to rise above your limitations to fulfill a larger mission in life. If your immediate response is, "I can't!" remember Jabez's prayer. Following its outline, make your requests to the Lord. And He will remove the shame of your past, replacing it with honor.

My prayer for divine ennoblement: _____

_____

_____

My prayer for divine enlargement: _____

_____

_____

My prayer for divine empowerment: _____

_____

_____

My prayer for divine enablement: _____

_____

_____

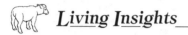

If you prayed in Study One for God's power and blessing in your life, then you need to ask yourself this question: "What larger sphere of influence does God want for me?" This question is not "How can I become more busy?" or "How can I squeeze more programs into my day?" Essentially, the question is: *What is my mission in life?*

What is your purpose for living? What singular, grand goal does God want for you? Now is your chance to seriously think about these questions. Evaluate what talents and resources God has already given you. Don't think about the negatives; those are behind you. Instead, take some time to write out your strengths.

_____

_____

_____

_____

Considering the gifts you have, what way can those strengths be used to accomplish a larger goal? Dream big! One man whose strengths were in business made it a goal to give away one million dollars by the time he retired. One young boy who cared for homeless people began collecting blankets for them. Now a warehouse is full of supplies for the needy. What seems impossible now can be possible through God. What is your impossible dream?

_____

_____

_____

_____

_____

Whether it is using your skills on the mission field or sharing the gospel with every neighbor on your street, God wants to bless you as you walk by faith to accomplish your holy ambition. Begin today!

BOOKS FOR
PROBING FURTHER

Dollhouses fascinate most little girls. They love to lift off the roof and decorate the tiny rooms, imagining miniature family dramas being enacted before their marveling eyes.

Throughout this study, we've approached the Old Testament like a dollhouse, in a sense. We've lifted off the roof and peeked into eight rooms, closely watching eight dramas. One man fought with his brother over here, and a father hugged his son over there. A wise woman saved her foolish husband in this scene, and a man fell desperately ill in another.

Before you place the roof back on this Old Testament house, take one final glance at the different stories and the principles they teach. Choose one or two of these lessons and determine to make some life changes as a result. To help you as you renovate those areas of your life, we have listed several resources under topical headings. May these books help you apply God's truths in your own family dramas.

Facing Giants

Swindoll, Charles R. *David: A Man of Passion and Destiny*. Dallas, Tex.: Word Publishing, Inc., 1997.

Parenting

Rice, Wayne, and David R. Veerman. *Understanding Your Teenager*. Dallas, Tex.: Word Publishing, Inc., 1999.

Disappointment in Marriage

Matteson, Richard, and Janis Long Harris. *What If I Married the Wrong Person?* Minneapolis, Minn.: Bethany House Publishers, 1996.

Stanley, Scott, Daniel W. Trathen, and B. Milton Bryan. *A Lasting Promise: A Christian Guide to Fighting for Your Marriage*. San Francisco, Calif.: Jossey-Bass, 1998.

Suffering

Smedes, Lewis B. *Shame and Grace: Healing the Shame We Don't Deserve*. San Francisco, Calif.: Harper San Francisco, 1994.

Tada, Joni Eareckson. *When God Weeps*. Grand Rapids, Mich.: Zondervan Publishing House, 2000.

Personal Struggles

Carter, Les. *Getting the Best of Your Anger*. Grand Rapids, Mich.: Baker Book House, 1997.

Smedes, Lewis B. *The Art of Forgiving: When You Need to Forgive and Don't Know How*. New York, N.Y.: Ballantine Books, 1997.

Some of the books listed above may be out of print and available only through a library. For those currently available, please contact your local Christian bookstore. Books by Charles R. Swindoll are available through Insight for Living. IFL also offers some books by other authors—please note the ordering information that follows and contact the office that serves you.

Ordering Information

Memorable Scenes from
Old Testament Homes

If you would like to order additional Bible study guides, purchase the audiocassette series that accompanies this guide, or request our product catalogs, please contact the office that serves you.

United States and International locations:

Insight for Living
Post Office Box 69000
Anaheim, CA 92817-0900

1-800-772-8888, 24 hours a day, seven days a week
(714) 575-5000, 8:00 A.M. to 4:30 P.M., Pacific time, Monday to Friday

Canada:

Insight for Living Ministries
Post Office Box 2510
Vancouver, BC, Canada V6B 3W7

1-800-663-7639, 24 hours a day, seven days a week
infocanada@insight.org

Australia:

Insight for Living, Inc.
20 Albert Street
Blackburn, VIC 3130, Australia

Toll-free 1800 772 888 or (03) 9877-4277, 8:30 A.M. to 5:00 P.M., Monday to Friday
iflaus@insight.org

World Wide Web:
www.insight.org

Bible Study Guide Subscription Program

Bible study guide subscriptions are available. Please call or write the office nearest you to find out how you can receive our Bible study guides on a regular basis.